scm centrebooks · six christia

Vernon Sproxton

Teilhard de Chardin

SCM PRESS LTD

334 01592 8
First published 1971
by SCM Press Ltd
56 Bloomsbury Street London
© SCM Press Ltd 1971
Printed in Great Britain by
Billing & Sons Ltd
Guildford and London

There is a grandeur in this view of life, with its several powers, having been originally breathed by the Creator into a few forms or into one; and that, whilst this planet has gone cycling on according to the fixed law of gravity, from so simple a beginning endless forms most beautiful and most wonderful have been, and are being evolved.

The closing words of
Darwin's *Origin of Species*, 1859

If progress is a myth – that is to say if, faced by the work involved, we can say: 'What's the good of it all?' – our efforts will flag. With that the whole of evolution will come to a halt – because we are evolution.

Teilhard de Chardin,
The Phenomenon of Man, 1959

Contents

Acknowledgments

Some of the material quoted in this book is accessible only in the form of typescript or duplicated notes, so there are no page references to *Le Coeur de la Matière*, *Le Christique*, and *Comment je Crois*. These and other materials have been made available through the courtesy of Mlle Jean Mortier, of the Fondation Teilhard de Chardin, in Paris. The short unacknowledged quotations in chapter 2 are taken mostly from *Writings in Time of War*, and *The Making of a Mind*; those in chapter 3 from *Letters from a Traveller*; and those in chapter 4 from *The Phenomenon of Man*. I am grateful to William Collins Sons & Co. Ltd for permission to quote these and the longer sections of the English translations of Teilhard's works. Rapp and Whiting Ltd have kindly allowed me to quote from *Letters to Two Friends*, and Burns & Oates Ltd from Cuénot's *Life of Teilhard*. Other quotations come from private conversations and correspondence with the people indicated.

Preface

This is a book about Teilhard for people who have heard of his name, but know little else about him. He has been known in English-speaking countries for more than a decade and people who have thought him significant will already know something of his struggles with the church and have read some of his works. I have therefore tried to achieve a straightforward narrative which, whilst telling the story of his life, at the same time introduces the reader to his main ideas. There are always new things to be found out and told about any great person, and readers already conversant with Teilhard's story may find some here; but the book is not intended to be 'A New View of Teilhard'. Moreover, whilst from time to time I take up a position with which other writers will not agree, it is not offered as a tract in the Teilhard debate.

Some readers may think that too much space has been devoted to the earlier periods. (A chapter for the four years of World War I, and only one chapter for the twenty years of China!) They may well be right. But there are, I think, four good reasons for so doing, and reasons of which Teilhard would have approved.

The importance of time is not its length, but what happens during that length. There is, as we shall see, *ticker-time* and *quality-time*. And there were phases in Teilhard's life when a great deal of personality-formation went on during a relatively short period.

The evolution of a mind follows the laws which trace the development of an organism, and to understand it properly and see what makes it work we have to examine its environment: its physical, cultural and spiritual habitat and the way in which it reacts to the varied elements which help to make up its setting in history.

There is also 'the heresy of paraphrase' (Cleanth Brooks) and this is particularly appropriate to *potted* Teilhard. Something of his 'taste' for life is lost if, during his critical years, he is not allowed to speak for himself.

And lastly, the earlier periods are of capital importance, because there we are given a glimpse of Teilhard wrestling with his thoughts and trying to make them yield some coherent idea; we are therefore able to see his thought in the process of formation.

To Teilhard palaeontology, geology and travel were the stuff of life. Their importance must not be minimized, but it is easy to lose what is essential about him in the minutiae of his craft (which, in any case, were highly technical) and an itinerary of his globe-trotting. Instead I have tried to give some account of a few important stages in his life with some suggestions of what lay behind them, together with some cameos of his influence on other people.

His impact on people was remarkable. I never knew him, but I have met many people who did: relatives, friends, colleagues, and students. And I have met many others who also never knew him personally but whose lives have been transformed by reading his books. It may or may not be true that the only people who are convinced by his arguments are those who want him to be right. But there is no doubt that many thinking men and women who were trapped between a Christianity which was out of touch with the vital forces of the modern world and a nihilism which betrayed their deepest intuitions, have found their way back to religion, and have acquired a new 'zest for life', by what his vision has led them to see.

I am not myself a thorough-going Teilhardian though I think – as I shall try to show – that what he was saying cannot be ignored. And I should be less than honest if I did not admit to the reader that in my view the man looms larger than the message.

Finally, I should like to thank those people who have been particularly helpful and encouraging to me during the writing of this short book: Lady Collins, of William Collins, who pioneered the publication of Teilhard's work in Britain, Mrs Kenneth Croose-Parry, the indefatigable Secretary of the Teilhard de Chardin Association, Mademoiselle Jeanne Mortier of the Fondation Teilhard de Chardin in Paris, and Canon F. W. Dillistone; my indebtedness to other biographers like Claude Cuénot and Robert Speaight, and interpreters like Emile Rideau and Henri de Lubac, is very great; and lastly to my assistant, Miss Patricia Miles, who has come to my rescue when I have been talking with people whose English is as bad as my French, who has translated sections of works not yet available in English, and who has winkled out as much jargon as she could.

Walton-on-Thames
November 1970

11

Introduction

In 1959, exactly one hundred years after the publication of Darwin's *Origin of Species*, *The Phenomenon of Man* appeared in English. Next to nothing was known about its author. A preface by Sir Julian Huxley, one of the greatest authorities on evolution, gave it some sort of scientific *nihil obstat:* 'a very remarkable book by a very remarkable human being'. It had already become a best-seller in France. 'Not since the twelfth century has there been such a satisfying exposition of the perfect understanding between the material world and that of Christ Incarnate' (*Figaro Littéraire*). Many reactions in Britain were just as enthusiastic. 'A landmark in thought. Possibly the book of the century' (*The Sunday Times*). 'This is a great book. If it is eclipsed by anything, it is by the spirit of the author, which shines through it' (*The Observer*). 'One of the most impressive books this century has seen' (*Religion in Education*). I seem to have been pretty impressed by it myself, for at the time I wrote in *Education;* 'Every so often a book appears which is destined to have an influence out of all proportion to the author's intention: Darwin's *Origin of Species*, Karl Marx's *Das Kapital*. Such a book may be *The Phenomenon of Man*.' If this sounded rather heady I should be forgiven, for even some secular philosophers, like Bernard Williams, found it engaging: 'Even if one disagrees, even if one thinks Father Pierre's metaphysical undertaking is necessarily impossible, one should read this book. It contains in its central chapters a picture of evolution which has depth, assurance, and imaginative power, which must leave an indelible impression on anyone who takes the trouble to follow it. No one who has read Father Pierre on insects, their forms of life and limitations, will ever see them in quite the same way again' (*The Spectator*, 4 December 1949).

Bernard Williams here puts his finger on something which is critical for our understanding of the influence of Teilhard de Chardin, for having seen something of his vision we cannot look at the place of man in the universe in quite the same way again; however much we may try we can never completely get him out of our intellectual system. Scientific, theological and metaphysical doubts may arise, but the sense of wanting him to be right persists. He offers something which corresponds to a deep-felt need, and it is this which has almost turned his Idea into an industry!

Look at what has happened since his death in 1955 lifted the ban on the publication of his 'dangerous' writings. Yards and yards of shelf-space are taken up with books by and about him. The Jesuits keep an index of works concerning members of the Order. In 1957 there were some forty references to Ignatius, their founder, and four to Teilhard; in the decade that followed, Ignatius stayed at a steady forty per year, but in 1967 Teilhard logged three hundred. These were major works of appraisal and criticism. Countless newspaper and magazine articles should be added for good measure – including a special edition of *Paris Match*. There is nothing, as yet, on *Teilhard and the Polish Problem*, but when you look at the other subjects you feel that it is only a matter of time! For he is compared with Jung, Marx, Freud, Darwin, Augustine, and other 'great barons of the mind'.

Attached to the Paris Museum of Natural History there is the Teilhard Foundation which employs a full-time staff who collect and collate Teilhardiana. In its library you will find scholars of every nation and every denomination. In many countries there are Teilhard Associations devoted to exploring his ideas and taking them further. They organize study groups, publish books, show films, and promote conferences on subjects of the greatest importance. His

13

influence extends to every country in the world, including Russia and Japan. No religious thinker of modern times has caught on in quite this way. Many who have been in the field for much longer, like Barth and Bultmann, are still virtually unknown beyond the theological élite.

Yet he is a curiously divisive force. Some scientists believe his influence to be pernicious. In 1961 the normally staid and prosaic pages of the philosophical journal *Mind* flowed with gall when Sir Peter Medawar wrote a critical notice of *The Phenomenon of Man* – regarded by its author as being of such fundamental importance that it was included in his collection of essays, *The Art of the Soluble*. In language vibrating with vituperative invective Medawar accused Teilhard of deceiving others by a deliberate willingness to be deceived himself. It was not surprising that Teilhard should put up Medawar's blood-pressure because in his Reith lectures (1959) he had shown his distaste for thinkers who ranged beyond narrow specialization with 'mopings or exaltations of poetistic prose'. Another distinguished British biologist, John Maynard Smith, dismisses Teilhard as a maker of myths. Yet scientists of equal distinction – and by no means all religious ones – look upon Teilhard as a creative thinker of first class importance: Dobzhansky, in America, author of *The Biology of Ultimate Concern*, Thorpe in Britain, and Piveteau in France.

In Britain, Bernard Towers, an anatomist specializing in embryology, took issue with Medawar,[1] and showed that the history of science proves that for its proper development it needs both the *master* who has a vast knowledge of a limited field, falling within an accepted framework of ideas, and *pioneers* who introduce new concepts of great daring and originality. He went on to prove that now-accepted scientific ideas have been resisted, initially, from within the scientific establishment, and showed how the philosophers of science have long ago exploded the myth that new scientific ideas spring from inductive processes alone. Bernard Towers holds that Teilhard used his master's position (as a specialist

14

in a very narrow field) as a platform from which to proclaim his original, his pioneering, Idea. In any event he shows that the pro- and anti-Teilhardians divide on other than scientific grounds.

Marxists, too, have frequently responded positively to Teilhard's ideas. In him they recognize a progressive Christian with whom they can enter into useful dialogue. Roger Garaudy, who got himself expelled from the Communist party because he consistently criticized the undialectical nature of the French Communist 'line', found that he and Teilhard share common ground: the need of the age for a philosophy based on creative development.

> ... Teilhard de Chardin presented his church, and, even further, all men of our own time, with a fundamental problem, ... the very problem which Marx raised for the first time a hundred years ago, and for the solution to which he provided the first elements: how are we to think of what is emerging for the future and control it?
> ... Teilhard recalled a fundamental aspect of Christianity which has often been obscured by later Platonism, that to progress towards God does not mean that one must turn one's back on the world: on the contrary, each man shares fully in his own transformation and construction, with all that is clearest in his thought, most urgent in his action, and most powerful in his passion.[2]

Here Garaudy spells out the need, though often inarticulate, to which Teilhard's thinking catered. Its place in time is important. His writings became available when a ruined world showed no signs of producing the spirit necessary for its renaissance. The twentieth century had been strewn with the wrecked shrines of secular gods that failed. The existentialism of the immediate post-war years was an existentialism of despair. (It could not speak of man's nature, but only of his condition. 'Man is what he is' – without purpose and without a goal.) It was bred not only of the immediate chaos but also of the long-term prospects for mankind, whose ultimate annihilation in icy waste was predicted by the laws of science. The obverse side of the despair was an anxiety almost equivalent to the brooding 'second religiousness' by which Oswald Spengler character-

15

ized the end of an age. The thorough-going *faithism* of the continental theologians appeared to be cynical about what could be done with the natural order and pronounced judgment on all historical processes. To be sure there was evidence of doomsday in the ruined cities and the haunting threat of a nuclear Armageddon in which Promethean man would use his new-found fire to set up hell on earth. Arthur Koestler, the disillusioned Marxist, caught the mood of many people when he asked whether there was no alternative between the Yogi, immured in a world of pure spirit, and the Commissar trapped in a mundane movement from which mercy had to be excluded. 'Perhaps a new God is going to be born?' But who was the prophet of the new God in whom ultimate meaning ran parallel with the natural development of the world, who held in creative tension the world of nature and the world of grace (science and religion), and who could bring back hope to the processes of history?

Teilhard filled the bill. He is frequently ill-served by the uncritical adulation of his followers. Many eccentric groups – like anthroposophists – try to get in on his act. But there can be no doubt that his Idea of the World as a Whole and Man as One draws attention to the fatally divisive nature of contemporary culture, cuts down to size all sorts of pompous specialization, and gives us *at worst* a noble Royal Lie. As he said at the end of *The Phenomenon of Man*, 'I may have gone astray at many points. It is up to others to do better.'

NOTES

1. *The Listener*, 29 December 1959. Cf. *Mind*, January 1961.
2. *Marxism in the Twentieth Century*, pp. 159–60.

1 'Auvergne moulded me'

Let us begin by getting his name right. It is pronounced *tayahr*, not *tailhard*, or *tile-hard*. And it is his surname. So it is quite wrong to refer to him as de Chardin, an adornment which came from his mother's side of the family. At his baptism he was given several names, but people knew him as Pierre Teilhard.

He came from the Auvergne. That says a great deal – like saying that a man is a highlander. Auvergnats tend to be proud, frugal, and independent. They have shown a marked taste for nonconformity. In the fifteenth century many of them embraced Calvinism, and harsh measures were used to discourage them. They had also a lot of sympathy with *la Fronde* (the sling), the popular movement of the seventeenth century which tried to slay the Goliath of centralized bureaucracy. So independence of mind is in their blood. It gives them drive and an urge to make good.

Many people look for the cause of these characteristics and find it in the geography of the region. They may be right. You could say of the Auvergnats – and of the Scots – what Lord Acton said of the Prussians: that they had to be industrious, because they were always conscious of the fact that Providence had not been very kind to them. In any case, Auvergne is critical for an understanding of Teilhard because it gave him the first glimpse of his greatest love, earth.

Auvergne forms part of the western range of the Massif Central in Central France. Its spectacular scenery ranges from the lush, florid meadows on the banks of the Allier to the range of burnt-out volcanoes which is crowned by the

Puy de Dôme. The terrain cannot have changed much since it cooled after having heaved, and bubbled, and burst during the great European cataclysm known as the Age of the Great Foldings. That was fifty million years ago. Climb to the top of the Puy de Dôme and look east. You are met with a prospect of almost primeval desolation which would make a suitable setting for a space-drama. As the mist lifts it reveals a landscape pock-marked with craters, fifty or sixty of them, craters within craters, and earthy gumboils which could not get up a big enough head of steam to burst. The early light sheds a grey-green pallor over everything. There are no trees. No sound reaches so high. The silence is eerie. If it is broken by an aeroplane, or if a creature, like a stray dog, wanders into the picture, neither seems in place. The sudden shock gives you the impression of being pushed forward several millenia. Hours, centuries, epochs seem like the flicker of an eye. You find yourself thinking in geological aeons.

Go down to the plateau two thousand feet below, but still three thousand feet above sea-level. See how inescapable is the Puy de Dôme. It dominates the region for miles around, even when your back is turned. Undoubtedly it rises from the surrounding land, but it rises so steeply that in a curious way it seems to be independent of it. It is like a strong, green god, brooding, its cone generally wreathed in cloud, sometimes flaming in the sunset. It dwarfs everything. The churches, flats, and factories of Clermont–Ferrand are made to look like dinky-toys. This great volcanic pile affirms that nature is supreme. Contemplate it for any length of time and you find yourself reaching for the adjectives by which Rudolph Otto described *the numinous*: magnificent, tremendous, fascinating. You begin to understand why primitive man venerated mountains. They cut you down to size. They induce a silent awe. That is half-way to worship.

This, then, was Teilhard's first habitat for, two-thirds of the way down the Puy de Dôme, and tucked into one of the folds of the west face, is Sarcenat, and the house where he was born. It is a large, rambling place, more like a small château than a house, with its turrets, casements, fountained-lawns and tree-lined drives. The immediate environs are poor: a few small cottages, and some open land reminiscent of Switzerland. Here the peasants graze their cattle and tend their family fruit-trees. A winding road runs through them to Orcines, a nondescript village with a gloomy parish church, where the priest will show you a prayer-stool inscribed *Teilhare*. With a little bit of encouragement he will produce the baptismal register which shows that Marie-Joseph-Pierre Teilhard de Chardin was born on 1 May 1881.

The Teilhards had another house in Clermont which they used during the winter. The older people in Orcines still remember how the horse-drawn carts, piled high with wicker linen-baskets, would rumble down from Sarcenat to the town. Clermont is also the birth-place of another French scientist and mystic, Blaise Pascal. Teilhard must often have passed Pascal's birth-place – no longer standing – on his way to Notre Dame du Port, where his family worshipped, and where many of them are buried. Notre Dame du Port is amongst the oldest of the churches of the Auvergne, but the town is dominated by a Gothic cathedral. It is constructed from stone quarried in the nearby mountains, a rich, brown-grey lava, the colour of pigeons' wings. Its twin towers are enormously high; Pascal confirmed his Puy de Dôme barometer experiments from them. The west door is a symphony of sculpture, and projects in stone the faith which Teilhard was taught to accept without question. From the pinnacle of the eaves the avenging angel peers down, sword already drawn, about to strike. To the right and left are the twelve apostles, expressions of frozen wonder on their faces. The typanum dramatically depicts the felicitious reception awaiting the elect in heaven and the horror awaiting those who are destined for the other place. But the spectator struggling up the straight boulevard which leads to the cathedral square is almost hypnotized by a massive and majestic Christ hewn out of a block of fine pumice. This

19

graphically represents the task which Teilhard was to set himself: tracing the lineaments of the Christ in solid rock.

You could say that the cone of the Puy de Dôme and the towers of the cathedral are the symbols of Teilhard's habitat, the two foci round which his whole life was to revolve, one of them representing the world of nature, and the other the world of grace. He was fortunate in having parents who could share his enthusiasm and encourage his passion for the exploration of both spheres.

Pictures of his father, Emmanuel, reveal a tall, handsome, rather Edwardian-looking man, who might have passed for an English gentleman-farmer. He was what the French call *un honnête homme*, which means something more than a built-in reluctance to cheat his income-tax returns. He had acquired a measure of prosperity but had enough free time to devote to the cultivation of taste in the arts and a sensibility to what was happening in the world of culture. He looked after his estates, pursued his flair for history by doing monumental work in the archives of Mont Ferrand, and was secretary of the local branch of the Academie des Sciences et des Arts. He read widely and had a great respect for Dickens. He was a fairly quiet – almost taciturn – man, but he could be given to bouts of genuine gaiety, and he possessed a mordant wit. There is not much evidence that religion played a vital part in his life. At heart he was probably a liberal humanist on nodding terms with the Catholic faith. Each evening he appeared for family prayers, raced through the *Pater Noster*, and slipped quickly away to his library for reading or a game of whist. Though he employed a governess to teach his children some subjects, he directed their reading, and was responsible for their Latin. He also taught them to take a deep interest in natural history, and to collect specimens for their home museum.

Pierre caught from his father a taste for the exact sciences as well as 'a certain balance upon which everything else rests'. He found in the environs of Sarcenat a ready-made nature reserve. Even today, when artificial fertilizers have destroyed so much insect life, you may lie on the lawns in front of the old house and be totally occupied in observing butterflies, moths and birds. But young Teilhard did not rank biological specimens amongst the highest of his 'joys of discovery'. That place was reserved for his most precious possession, which still exists: a collection of rocks and pebbles. Auvergne is a happy-hunting ground for the geologist and from an early age Pierre was completely captivated by stones. Why, it is not easy to say. It might even have had something to do with his Christian name. People have been prompted to do things by less than a name. But it is likely that he was looking for something which transcended even the rocks.

To his mother, Berthe, who came from Picardy, he said he owed the better part of his soul. If his father fostered his interest in the world of nature, his mother led him gently into the life of grace. When she died, in 1936, he said that it was she who had encouraged his devotion to the Sacred Heart and struck the spark which lit up 'his universe'. 'It was, without any doubt, through my mother, and drawn from the main stream of Christian mysticism, that this spark illuminated and inflamed my child soul. . . . With my mother's milk a supernatural sense of the divine flowed into me side by side with the "natural" sense of plenitude.'[1] When, years later, he coined several new concepts to express his attitude to life, his mother's devotion was included naturally in his world-view.

By all accounts she was a woman of more than ordinary piety. She rose early in the morning – often before dawn – and walked two miles across the fields to hear Mass at Orcines; and she was back home in time to prepare breakfast for the family. She was completely self-effacing, and gave up much of her time to charity. She created a style of family life based on a deep personal faith and guarded by a sensible discipline. Such a cultivated, comfortable, and secure home naturally protected Teilhard against exposure to the great amount of poverty and suffering which surrounded him, but the give-and-take of a large family made excellent training for the corporate life he was to lead for the rest of his life.

Middle-class comfort could do nothing to prevent the family being afflicted by what Teilhard came to know as 'the forces of diminishment'. Six of the eleven children died before reaching middle age. This experience tempered and deepened the faith of his mother. It caused Teilhard to search for the durable. 'My very first memory is of my mother clipping off a few of my curls. I picked one up and held it to the fire. It was burned up in a flash. Terrible grief overcame me. I learned that I was perishable.'[2]

The transitoriness of human life appalled him. He was always on the look-out for something constant. One day he came across the share-spanner of an old plough. It became his talisman. He put it in a secret place and from time to time would make a tryst with his *genie de fer*. 'In all my childish experience there was nothing in the world higher, more durable than this wonderful substance.' But after being absent for some time he returned to find that it had oxidized and was beginning to crumble. When he discovered that even iron rusted and disintegrated he broke down and cried. Even then he was seeking an Idea which would embrace his own frail mortality and the constancy of solid rock. He was then seven years old.

II

When he was eleven he was sent to a boarding-school at Notre Dame de Mongré, Villefranche. All the Teilhard boys went there as a matter of course. (The girls were educated at Clermont with the Ursulines.) In those days Mongré was run by the Jesuits and specialized in breeding young men of the officer class. Indeed the buildings could easily be mistaken for barracks. Even today the décor is heavy and forbidding; the quadrangles, with their ambulatories, give the impression that the place is turned in on itself. Gloomy black and gilt honours boards proclaim the names of those boys who in their day did well. One of them is topped by

Teilhard. Not that he was a genius, but he did well in most subjects, and revealed a marked inclination towards the sciences. His worst subject was religious knowledge, or at least that part of Catholic religious instruction which is dressed up in saccharine saintliness. There was a lot of it. Teilhard found it distasteful. 'All those goody-goody saints; who on earth would want to spend eternity with that lot!'

Yet even at that age he seems to have been able to discern the essence of the faith behind the gaudy trappings. He appears to have been untroubled by any fundamental doubts, and subsequently made his act of consecration to Our Lady. His devotion to the Sacred Heart of Jesus was never to leave him. His peers were quick to recognize in this lanky, exemplary scholar, the beginnings of an extraordinary piety. They elected him to be secretary and then prefect of the Sodality of the Immaculate Conception. An entry he made in the minutes of the Sodality hints at the shape of things to come:

Our director . . . gave us a talk full of originality but very much to the point. He said that the best way for us to show our love for the Blessed Virgin is to try to be men with a sense of duty, that is Christians. Then, when we leave school, we can really work to bring France back to the road God has mapped out for it, and make it Christian again. If we do this we shall give back to Mary one of the brightest jewels in her crown.[3]

Ever since the seventeenth century rationalism had gradually been corroding the solder which had kept *Gallia* in the Virgin's crown. It had toppled out over a hundred years before Teilhard's time, and neither the wit nor the wiles of the Jesuits had been able to put it back again. France became, what she essentially remains, a secular state, rife with an anti-clericalism which was going to make the going hard for religious orders. It was therefore no soft option which Teilhard chose when in 1897 he wrote to his parents, 'It seems to me that God is offering me a vocation to leave the world. You can well imagine that once I'm certain that I am not mistaken, I shall answer the call; and

23

I know, too, that you will be the last to raise any difficulties.'

They made no difficulties, of course; and he soon became certain that he had a vocation to enter the Society of Jesus; not because he had been at one of their schools, but because he was looking for 'the perfect' in the world of the spirit as he had been looking for 'the permanent' in the world of matter. Indeed, whilst this quite clear call out of the world was echoing in his soul, a perceptive observer had noted that an equally irresistible call to the earth had been forming in his mind. One – perhaps the brightest – of his teachers was Henri Bremond. Bremond was at this time one of the rising stars in the Jesuit firmament. His influence on the young Teilhard is a matter of speculation, but it cannot have been small. For one thing, he had some radical ideas about teaching, allowing pupils to follow their natural interests; and this at a time when the Order banned anything that looked like Froebelism. Moreover, he was a man of wide-ranging interests, and he was constantly in touch with progressive religious ideas, especially in England. He was fascinated by people like Newman and Pusey; and not only thinkers in the Catholic tradition, but nonconformists as well: the Caird Brothers and Fairbairn. Dr Alexander Whyte was his 'venerable friend'. Wesley fascinated him. Having cast away the blinkers of Jesuit religious thinking he no doubt absorbed much of the critical attitudes of secular thought of the period by a kind of intellectual osmosis. Some of this must have brushed off on to his pupils before his 'modernist' opinions forced him to quit the Order. Several of them who later became famous spoke of the great debt they owed him and his critical method, 'a criticism that anticipated success instead of following it'. But at the level of literature he and Pierre Teilhard never really 'clicked'.

Thirty years ago, one of my classical pupils was a little fellow from Auvergne, very intelligent, first in every subject, but disconcertingly well-behaved. The most backward and thick-skulled members of the class occasionally came alive; their eyes would light up when they were given something more thrilling to read or something more exciting to do. But he, never; and it was only later that I learned the the secret of his seeming indifference. Transporting his mind far away from us was another, a jealous and absorbing passion – rocks.[4]

Perhaps it was 'only long afterwards' – or, indeed during the time when he was Teilhard's professor at Aix – that Teilhard latched on to some of Bremond's insights. For a friend of Bremond describing the last days of Bremond could easily have been describing the older Teilhard. 'He opens his window on to the terrace; we lean out silently, the evening glory making us forget the literary life and its charming puppets. Then he talks to me of the glory of the world. Ah! his shade which floats, light and incorruptible, around me reminds me of nothing else.'[5]

This, as I said, is speculation. What is certain, on the testimony of Bremond, is that whilst he was at school Teilhard's heart was still in Auvergne. At the end of his school-days it was to Auvergne that he returned. The spartan life of Mongré had left him run-down and anaemic, so he did not enter his novitiate straight away. During the week he spent his time with tutors preparing for his baccalauréat in mathematics. On Sundays he was up amongst the puys gathering specimens. He was also forming what was to become one of the deepest relationships of his life. In their childhood spent together at Clermont Ferrand Marguerite Teilhard-Chambon had already discovered a soul-affinity with cousin Pierre.

III

As Brother Pierre he started his training for entry to the Society of Jesus at Aix-en-Provence. By any standards it was long and arduous – fourteen years altogether. It was also unbelievably conservative. In 1864 Pius IX had issued the *Syllabus of Errors*. This claimed for the church complete control over men's ideas: science, culture, education – everything. It served to aggravate the mood of anti-clericalism. Far from diminishing, it tended to foster an interest in some of the more dangerous facets of modernism, like Darwinism and biblical-criticism. It was a time when all good Catholics were called upon to bury their heads in the sand. Naturally the state dug in its heels. Politicians interpreted the syllabus as an all-out declaration of war on the things for which the Republic stood: democratic processes, and the spirit of science. Many of them were free-thinkers. They looked more to science than to faith for the inspiration and direction needed to construct a new society. The control of the church over the thinking of the young stood in the way of achieving this goal. Over a couple of decades priestly power in education was gradually reduced. Members of religious orders were prevented from teaching in the *lycées*. In 1882 all state education was 'laïcised'. This meant that priests were not allowed to teach (except after school-hours and off the premises) and that there had to be a complete divorce between education and religious ideas. The climax was reached in 1901 when the incarnation of anti-clericalism, Emile Combes, came to power and the religious orders were expelled from France.

So, just as he began the second stage of his training at Laval, Teilhard had literally to take to his heels. The Jesuits found hospitality in Britain, mainly at Hastings and Canterbury. But Teilhard's group turned up in Jersey. They had to travel in disguise: in motoring caps, morning coats, old green bowlers, and tails. They must have looked grotesque. But photographs show that Teilhard was never much of a one for clothes.

IV

The British Isles had a considerable influence, and encouraged in Teilhard a growing determination to spend his life investigating the 'stuff' of earth. They were also the setting of some of his emotional and spiritual turning-points.

In Jersey the novices found accommodation in a converted seaside hotel. Teilhard found it even less attractive than either his teachers or his method. He had little taste for the logic-chopping Aristotelianism which seemed to have all the right answers for all the wrong questions. And his fellow-students – amongst whom he made one or two life-long friends – were just as restless. He lost no opportunity of escaping from the airy speculations of his mentors to find the comfort of the too, too solid earth: the rocks and fossils of the Jersey coast. With the help of a colleague he wrote a paper on the geology of the island which was published in *The Bulletin of the Jersey Society*.

He found himself attracted to physics. (It was pre-Quantum physics, of course, though Max Planck had elaborated his theory several years previously.) He made a vow that one day he would wrest from nature the secret of gravity. Matter bemused him. He was so obsessed by it that the earthly world was exerting a greater pull on him than the spiritual one to which his vows had committed him. There was a crisis of vocation. In an agony of worry he confessed to the novice-master that his passion for rocks was distracting his mind from preparation for the priest-hood. The novice-master was reassuring. He told him that God looked just as much for the proper development of his natural talents as for the perfection of his soul. This was perceptive advice. But the action which followed shortly afterwards was even wiser. Teilhard was sent off to Egypt to teach physics at the College of the Holy Family in Cairo.

The time spent in Egypt – three years or so – did a great deal for Teilhard in several different ways. It gave him breathing space at a time when he was having to make adjustments in his response to life. It allowed him the 'distance' to come to terms with what he later described as 'the forces of diminishment'. His eldest brother had died as Teilhard came to Jersey. Shortly afterwards his twelve-year-old sister, Louise, died of meningitis, and another sister, Marguerite, became a permanent invalid after an attack of pleurisy. These events grieved him, but they did not over-whelm him. His letters to his parents show that his spiritual sensitivities had been in no way blunted by his preoccupation with matter. Indeed, from his correspondence with

27

Marguerite (Guigite) some of his finest devotional writing was to come.

But Egypt did much more than help him to overcome his sadness. It got him away from the turned-in, stuffy atmosphere of the seminary. It offered him vastly wider horizons than anything he had known before. It allowed him to enlarge his knowledge of archaeology. The Middle East induced a romantic wanderlust which was never to leave him. In making contact with cultures palpably different from and older than his own he was able to perceive fresh historical perspectives. The new vistas, both vertical and horizontal, helped him to evolve a concept of the world as a single whole, though the discovery of its vital energy had to wait until he returned to England.

Above all, perhaps, he was able to try his hand at teaching. He appears to have relished it. Apart from anything else it helped him to clarify the meaning of 'truths only half understood'. Jesuits are essentially teachers and most of the Jesuits who appear in the Teilhard story are no exception; but they teach almost anything but religion. Protestants find this idea difficult to understand. It is more comprehensible if the missionary nature of the Order of Jesus is kept in mind. The Order was founded to out-think and out-teach paganism on the one hand and protestantism on the other. The most effective way of sustaining that mission was to teach, to get hold of the child when young and teach him the truths of religion and everything else as well. There have been black pages written in Jesuit history in the past centuries and, as we shall see, some blotched ones in the present. But Europe would be a very different place – and I cannot believe a better one – if all the days and years of Jesuit teaching were withdrawn. Be that as it may, the Jesuit emphasis on teaching explains why it is customary in France to see a white-coated cleric hemmed in by all the paraphernalia of a chemistry laboratory. It also explains why when he was in Egypt Teilhard found nothing inconsistent with his religious beliefs when he began to see that his future vocation might find fulfilment in teaching the physical sciences.

When he returned to England it was to Ore Place at Hastings, the centre for theological instruction. It was whilst he was here that Teilhard 'got' evolution, 'got' it in the way that some young men 'get' religion. He was then in his late twenties and restless. Though he never seems to have doubted the truth of the Catholic faith, it clearly did not provide him with the master-principle he needed to key-together the ideas which were forming in his mind. At this stage his life is reminiscent of the young Kierkegaard, in revolt against the complacency of Danish Christianity, wandering in a state of confusion along the cliff at Gilleleje, and writing in his diary, 'the thing is to find a truth which is true *for me*, to find *the idea for which I can live and die*'.[6] Like Kierkegaard, Teilhard felt that contemporary Christianity did not provide the answer to his deepest intuitions and profoundest questions. It was certainly not forthcoming from theology, or from those who taught him of whom, for the most part, he spoke without enthusiasm. This is not surprising. Like most Catholic seminaries, Ore Place tended to be untouched by biblical criticism. Its teaching on creation was entirely devoted to the propagation of *fixisme*, the biological theory that living species were always the same and not subject during their creation to the forces of evolution. No wonder Teilhard seized with relief on 'evolution', not merely as an intellectually attractive theory, but as the dominating emotional factor in that period of his life. When he looked back on his days at Hastings, this above all was what he remembered.

All that I can remember from that time is the extraordinary effect of density and intensity which the English countryside had upon me – especially at sunset when the Sussex woods seemed to be bursting with all the fossil life I sought among the cliffs and quarries of the Weald's clay. And through all this the magic word 'evolution' echoed ceaselessly in my mind, like a refrain, a promise, a call. At times it seemed as though a universal Being would suddenly take shape in nature before my eyes. . . . It was during these days that, little by little, more as a Presence than an abstract idea, I became aware from within of a profound total movement of the whole universe around me.[7]

The cynic might be inclined to say that he was going through a Keatsian period – only ten years later than most young men. Robert Bridges, roaming over the South Downs, had the same feeling: 'This spiritual elation and response to nature is man's generic mark.'[8] Certainly he himself found the experience puzzling. 'Under what influence or shock or by what steps did this feeling appear and put down such deep roots in me?' We know that at the time he had been reading Bergson's *Creative Evolution* which was published in 1907. It seems incredible that a young man from a cultured home should have to wait until he was nearly thirty before stumbling on 'evolution'. A century had passed since his compatriot, Lamarck, had set out his theory of 'transformisme'. Etienne St Hilaire had also prepared the minds of Frenchmen for the new idea. Mendel, Charles Darwin, T. H. Huxley were all dead by this time. That Teilhard should have been proof against their revolutionary thinking at least testifies to the efficiency of the mental blinkers in which Rome was able to put her nascent intellectuals.

Be that as it may, Bergson's philosophy corresponded to Teilhard's need. Moreover, it introduced him to a whole set of ideas which were then maturing amongst French philosophers. These acted as a matrix in which his own idiosyncratic concepts could be formed. For though he had been cut off from the main stream of secular French culture, he was preoccupied with some of the same problems.

In the eighteenth century France was the setting of a massive assault on the church as the redoubt of dogma, superstition, and mental jiggery-pokery. The *Enlightenment*, starting with Descartes, sustained by Voltaire, and crowned by Comte, rhapsodises over the power of human reason. It resulted in *positivism*, the notion that the only certain truths are those of observable phenomena; that is, those that can be tested by scientific methods. The upshot of this movement was the production of a new kind of orthodoxy, which was just as ready as the Old Faith to cry, 'infidel'.

The end of the nineteenth century was the great period of intellectual seed-sowing which was to flower in the twentieth. Marx, Darwin, Freud, Nietzsche, the four thinkers who have radically altered our 'world-view' date from this time, though in France their influence was probably beamed through 'prismatic thinkers' like Georges Sorel. And in France, positivism – aided by anti-clericalism – began to win the day until, inevitably, a reaction set in, and a movement began which tried to come to terms with the new ideas without selling-out to materialism. The attack on the stronghold of positivism was an attempt to liberate 'spirit', and 'freedom'. It tried to destroy the purely mechanical view of nature and replace it by some sort of free process. 'Natural science may be all right in its own sphere,' the critics of positivism said, in effect, 'but it does not exhaust reality as a whole. There are realms of being which it is not equipped to investigate. Moreover, it depends for its very life on freedom. Given its methods science may not be able to detect "spirit" in nature; yet its very existence is a tribute to the free spiritual activity of the scientist'.

'Science is a system of symbols which gives us a usable representation of realities we are unable to know directly. The existence and properties of these symbols can only be known by an original activity of the spirit.'[9] That is a quotation from the Gifford Lectures delivered in Glasgow in 1904 by the French philosopher, Emile Boutroux. It is important, not simply because some of his concepts come very close to those of Teilhard, but because the title of the lectures, *Nature and Spirit*, together with some of the subjects he covers, reveals the 'feel' of the spirit philosophers: Chance and Freedom, The Contingency of Natural Laws, Certainty or Truth, Science and Culture. In *De la Contincence des Lois de la Nature*, he writes about the power of psychic energy to organize new qualities of being.

Moreover, the reconciliation of science and religion, an

idea which obsessed the young Teilhard, also preoccupied the old Boutroux. At the conclusion of an article he contributed to *The Cambridge Modern History* – he must have been writing at the turn of the century – he says:

> With Descartes philosophy properly so-called finds in human reason the common source of our knowledge of nature and our beliefs concerning the supernatural. With Gassendi . . . science tends to be self-sufficient, and to banish religion to the obscure retreat of individual feeling, till the time comes for expelling it altogether. With Pascal, the supreme guidance of reason, science, and nature is claimed by religion, on proving that it alone can solve the problem inherent in nature, science, and religion. Religion, science, reason – are not these the three teachers of humanity, the three powers that even today struggle for control of the moral world? And even today are we not asking ourselves which of these three is to overcome and subjugate the others – or whether they may be brought together in a lasting and beneficent harmony?[10]

This passionate plea in a work of academic history is a testimony to the restless ferment of ideas in which Teilhard's education took place. There was nothing unique about some of his concerns: the reconciliation of science and religion, the abolition of the matter *versus* spirit polarity. Other ideas in the air were about the methodology of social revolution, like Georges Sorel's 'audacious minority' as the spearhead of evolution. But in saying that there was nothing unique about many of his ideas, I am not suggesting that he was a plagiarist. It is clear that he had read little if anything of the seminal thinkers. (In any case, ideas have a habit of cropping up simultaneously in different places.) What I am trying to show is that his intellectual energy flowed from the tension between the two poles in his mental make-up: faith in revelation (the 'above') and – the opposite – secular evolutionary ideas (the 'ahead'). This was the genesis of his original idea. And the first thing he had to do was disinfect his mind of an assumption which both religion and science had led him to believe was unquestionable.

> Up to that point, education and religion had always led me into the unthinking and docile acceptance of the basic heterogeneousness

between Matter and Spirit, Body and Soul, Conscious and Unconscious: two substances of a different nature; two kinds of Being,
incomprehensibly joined together in the living Compound; and I was
assured that it was necessary to assert that the former (*my* divine
Matter) was only the humble servant (not to say adversary) of the
latter; but the latter (my Spirit) became somewhat low in my estima-
tion because of the fact that it was no more than a Shadow which
was supposed to be venerated on principle, and in which (emotionally
and intellectually speaking) I was in fact incapable of feeling any
lively interest at all. You may judge therefore what was the resulting
inner liberation and expansion of my being when, as I took my first
hesitant steps in an Evolutive world, I established that the dualism
in which I had been brought up was vanishing like a mist before the
rising sun. Matter and Spirit: not two things at all, but two *states*,
two faces of the same cosmic stuff.[11]

Poor Teilhard. You can see what a struggle he must have
had. The heterogeneity of body and spirit were fundamental
to Catholic teaching about man. And he found himself
having to destroy this foundation-stone before he could lay
his first brick.

V

There is no wonder, then, that Teilhard's letters from
England reveal that, though his study was theology, his
interest was captured by the terrain. Fortunately, the rector
of Ore Place was fairly liberal in outlook, and he allowed
Teilhard to make many geological excursions. He sent
specimens to the Natural History Museum in London. Some
of them carry his name. His status as a palaeontologist was
becoming more and more professional. Local amateur
geologists, like Charles Dawson, became his friends.
Dawson introduced him to Smith Woodward, the curator
of the Natural History Museum's geology department. They
heard that some gravel-diggers at Piltdown, near Uckfield,
in Sussex, had disinterred a human skull, crude flint tools,
and elephant fossils. They decided to excavate the site and
their work led eventually to the discovery of what later
became known as *Eonthrophus Dawsoni*, or Piltdown Man.
The find became the centre of a great controversy – a

palaeontological *cause célèbre*. English and French pre-historians were bitterly divided about his identity, but Teilhard came down on the side of Smith Woodward. For forty years a mystery surrounded Piltdown man. Then modern techniques proved conclusively that the whole affair had been a splendid hoax. When it was exposed Teilhard was glad because, by all the rules, Eoanthropus was a monster who should not have existed, but he was sorry that the discovery tarnished one of his earliest and most exciting scientific moments.

In the long, hot summer of 1911 Teilhard was ordained. His family came over for the ceremony. (They were in mourning. His elder sister, Françoise, the superior of an old people's home founded by the Little Sisters of the Poor, had died of smallpox in Shanghai.) The next day he celebrated his first Mass, his parents being his first communicants, the servers – his brothers Gabriel and Joseph.

The following year he returned to France to complete his scientific training at the Catholic Institute and the Collège de France. He went away on a number of digs but, more important than places at this stage, were two people whose acquaintance he made, both of them great names: the Abbé Henri Breuil, later called 'the pope of palaeontology', and Marcellin Boule, Professor of Palaeontology at the Paris Museum.

Like Teilhard, Boule was also an Auvergnat – a stocky, and outspoken man. Though he did not suffer fools gladly he was rarely wrong in his judgment about men. He soon summed up Teilhard's prospects as a naturalist and pronounced him well-equipped for a brilliant future. But he also detected another quality, 'valuable as it is rare, a combination of minute analysis, a gift of wide synthesis, and great independence of mind'. Teilhard's character had set firmly in the Auvergne mould. He was going to challenge categories of interpretation which had been accepted so far as normal. He would find a way of interpreting matter and spirit, heaven and earth, inanimate and human, in such a way that they did not centre in different Poles, but converged on a single Point. And this he would do as a priestly act. The main direction of his life was determined. He would not seek salvation by abandoning the world, but by immersing himself more and more in it and helping to *build the earth*.

NOTES

1. *Le Coeur de la Matière*, unpublished.
2. Ibid.
3. Cuénot, p. 5.
4. *Le Charme d'Athenes*, Henri Bremond, quoted by Speaight, p. 27.
5. Henry Hogarth, *Henri Bremond*, SPCK 1950, p. 156.
6. *The Journals of Søren Kierkegaard*, translated by Alexander Dru, OUP, p. 15. See also the previous day's entry on the spiritual dimensions of the natural world. Cf. also Coleridge's definition of the Idea. 'The maxim contains past knowledge and is retrospective and the Idea contains future knowledge and is prospective.'
7. *Le Coeur de la Matière*.
8. *The Testament of Beauty*, Book I, line 318. The whole of this work makes a fruitful comparison with Teilhard's metaphysical vision; especially Bridges' 'Orders' – atomic, organic, sensuous, self-conscient.
9. Boutroux: synopsis of his Gifford lectures in the University Library, Glasgow.
10. Volume IV, p. 759.
11. *Le Coeur de la Matière*.

2 'Baptism in the Real'

Earth next presented itself to Teilhard in the form of mud and flame. The mountains of the Auvergne had moulded him, but he was tempered by four years in the trenches of Flanders. 'Baptism in the real', is how he described the experience. This is the kind of expression which spreads despair amongst philosophers who try to make sense of Teilhard's language and find that his 'weasel words' continually slip from their grasp. To be sure, life in a seminary or a farmstead can be just as 'real' as life in the trenches; there is nothing essentially more 'real' about warfare than anything else.[2] But it is easy enough to see what he meant. For thirty years he had moved in fairly confined circles. Protected and sheltered by his home and school and later by his Order, he knew next to nothing of the rough-and-tumble of working-class life with its hardships and insecurities; and what he did know was as an outsider. He had rarely brushed up against people who did not share his sensibility and culture. Now he had to. Indeed, he wanted to. He was looking for the face of Humanity and he was suspected that he might discover it in Flanders just as in England he had found in nature the face of Universal Being.

Life lived cheek by jowl with men of different temperaments from varied social backgrounds and religious faiths gave him a sense of exaltation. The closely-woven tissues of human relationships brought him face to face with the hopes and fears of ordinary men. It was life with the nerve exposed, and it gave him an opportunity of testing the humanity in himself. He was completely committed to the war on its own grounds, as we shall see later. He was not using army life merely to enlarge his own experience and sharpen his own perception. But we know from his letters to his cousin and the notes he was making at the time that he was relating what was happening to him to his overriding idea: 'sacred evolution, the instrument of beatification'.

The outbreak of war found Teilhard in Paris. He had just returned, feeling extremely fit, from a climbing holiday in Grenoble. Having heard the declaration of general mobilization on 1 August 1914, he had come straight back as he wanted to be in the thick of things. He was already on the army reserve, but he had never seen active duty. When he tried to get into the ambulance service he was told to stay put and wait to be called. He did so, with ill-concealed impatience. At the end of September he was still waiting. Then he did receive orders – to return to Canterbury to begin his 'third year', a time of retreat for newly ordained Jesuits who have not yet taken their final vows. For a month he quietly contemplated the *Spiritual Exercise* of Ignatius. The silence had hardly been broken when he received news that his twenty-year-old brother, Gonzagues, had been killed at the front. He tried to comfort his parents by telling them that there could be no more beautiful ideal for their son than for him to give his life in 'one of the greatest tasks this century has seen'. These words show the way he was beginning to look upon the war, as a creative catastrophe of almost geological size and significance. By December he was playing a part in it himself.

At the beginning of 1915 he appeared at the front as a stretcher-bearer in a Moroccan light-infantry regiment. The soldiers were mostly Arabs. To make himself more at one with them he discarded the service-blue uniform and cap and in their place adopted their khaki and fez. The troops, both French and Arab, took him to themselves. He knew how to speak with them and was always sensitive to their needs. When they fell or were injured in battle they wanted 'Monsieur Teilhard' to be near them. The regiment was involved in some of the heaviest fighting of the war, notably

37

Verdun and the second battle of the Marne. Teilhard constantly lamented that his position as stretcher-bearer prevented him from going 'over the top' with the men, and he was always pained when the tally of losses was made. But, however small he may have thought his own contribution to the war to have been, his superiors and colleagues took a very different view. Within a few months he had won both the *Medaille Militaire* and the *Croix de Guerre*. When the war was over his regiment sent a proposal – backed by every rank – that he should be made a Chevalier of the Legion of Honour. In June 1920 the award was promulgated.

A day-to-day account of Teilhard's war experiences does not exist but, from his letters and the memoirs of a few comrades, it is possible to draw a few sketches of the soldier-priest. His activities clearly ranged beyond those of a stretcher-bearer, for he showed a great deal of concern for the general welfare of the men, several times asking his cousin to send such things as playing-cards and footballs. He was a pastor, too, carrying the Sacrament wherever he went. (Towards the end of 1915 he was relieved of some of his duties to free him for more spiritual tasks. Later still he was offered a commission but turned it down as he wanted only to stay with the men.) Occasionally, during lulls in the fighting, he would detach himself from the regiment to give some help to the local priest, relishing the thought of a night or two in a proper bed. He read a great deal, his cousin regularly posting journals to the front; and his reading covered a fairly wide spectrum, from Cardinal Newman at one end to *The Daily Mail* at the other. Any other spare time was spent in examining the fossils, bones, and strata that the entrenchments had laid bare. For though he wore the uniform of a soldier and as such discharged his duties with bravery and distinction, he was always at the same time both scientist and priest.

One of his officers gave this account of his courage:

Word came to Lt. Col. Vernois that Capt. Courtiaux was missing.

It seemed likely that he had perished under machine-gun fire if he had not been blown to bits by a shell. . . . Although an atheist he got on well with Teilhard. The Colonel, who wanted to make sure of Courtiaux's fate and to retrieve the body if possible, gave orders for a search-party, to be made up of volunteers. Teilhard, hearing of this, came to the Colonel to ask as a special favour to be allowed to go out alone and so spare a search-patrol the risk. The Colonel hesitated at first, but finally agreed. Whilst there was still light, they noted the spot where Courtiaux must have fallen – almost right in front of the German machine-gun post.

When it was dark, about ten it must have been, Teilhard crawled out on the field. Next morning, when you could just see light, he was back again with the body of Courtiaux over his shoulder. Our lines . . . can't have been more than two or three hundred yards from the Germans.[1]

The same officer also observed the priest's devotion when, at the beginning of 1916, the regiment took over part of the line in front of Passchendale. This was flat, swampy ground at the best of times, and incessant rain had turned it into a quagmire. The first two feet of earth was ooze, so trenches were out of the question. Primitive protection was made by shoring up old planks and logs with sandbags filled with soil from behind the lines. These huts gave some shelter from enemy fire, but they were a home-from-home for rats. Whilst huddling together in one of them a number of Frenchmen asked Teilhard to say Mass for their families. Shivering from cold, and crouching under the low roof, Father Teilhard and a congregation of six celebrated Mass. As he was putting away the vessels the Germans riddled the sector with bullets. None of the worshippers was hurt. Teilhard, 'in a calm and serious voice said, "I had still my blessing to give you. God being with us, did not wish one of us to be hit." With that he gave us his blessing and returned to his aid-post.'[2]

A Jesuit postulant, having taken simple vows, spends two years as a novice and then, after ordination, as a 'tertian' he spends another year before taking his final vows. In May 1918, in a ceremony not far from the lines, Teilhard took his solemn vows. 'War served as his tertianship' (Cuénot).

By far the most important aspect of Teilhard's war service was not his activity, but the 'within' of the experience. This ability to draw from such an unpromising environment the essential nourishment for both his spirit and his mind is virtually unique. There were certainly soldiers who turned their war-time life into splendid and moving literature which has ennobled our understanding of human nature. Few, if any, have shown Teilhard's capacity for sustained, concentrated, abstract thought. (One of his friends was astonished to discover that he had not given up philosophy for the duration!) For it was whilst he was a soldier that Teilhard constructed on the basis of his original Idea the outlines of an intellectual theory which, though it was to be modified, contained the key to everything he was later going to say about human destiny. It is clear from his correspondence (notably *The Making of a Mind*)[3] and his essays (*Writings in Time of War*) that there had already formed in his mind all the materials with which he would build his theory of the evolution of the world. It was perhaps another case of:

> Two men looked through prison bars,
> The one saw mud, the other stars.

It might well be said that Teilhard's buoyant optimism was starry-eyed for, shortly after Verdun, he was writing: 'Besides communion with God, and communion with Earth, there is a communion with God through Earth – the Earth becoming like a great Host in which God would be contained for us. I would like to be able to love Christ passionately (*by* loving) *in the very act* of loving the Universe.'[4]

This is taken from a very revealing letter which he despatched to a distinguished contemporary, a Jesuit biblical scholar. It shows, elsewhere, that he had still not quite resolved the crisis of vocation which had happened in Jersey and was still struggling to find a formula which would embrace 'this-worldliness and other-worldliness' in a single discipline. Clearly his mind was in a maelstrom, and he confesses that some of his ideas are vague. But with the advantage of hind-sight some things become transparent.

We can see from this letter what was really gnawing at his spirit. Quite simply it was main-line Catholic (and for that matter Protestant) teaching about the place of 'the world'. This is pointed up by such phrases as 'a vale of soul-making'. This is a view which regards the world as a stage or setting in which our own personal dreams and destinies are played out, without itself being the object of any transfiguration or change. It would be tempting to think that this view is on its way out, replaced by a much more realistic assessment of the place of the material world. At any rate we give lip-service to the idea by talking about incarnational theology, secular Christianity, and the celebration of worldliness. But, in both Catholicism and Protestantism, there is plenty of evidence to show that salvation depends on our removing ourselves from our bodily, historical situation and turning aside from our involvement in nature to that of pure Spirit in order to *hear the Word of God*. Now Teilhard was looking for a way of reconciling this kind of 'spiritual' detachment with a proper immersion not in matter as such (for we cannot escape *being in it*) but with the whole process of earthly progress. He accepted that there was some virtue in refining his soul by immersing himself in the abstract sciences, and that such a discipline – thinking God's thoughts after him – would evoke a divine blessing. But that was not enough. In fact it was totally to miss the point. He did not want to see the world merely as an opportunity of acquiring merit. He wanted to see it as an eternal creation in its own right, something to be built up and beautified. Believing that God himself lay hidden in the very stuff of the cosmic organism, which he and others loved, he realized that it was impossible to divorce the love of earth from its object. 'Cannot the object, the actual matter of our human

41

passions be transfigured, transformed into the Absolute, the definitive, the divine. I believe it can.' To the very core of his being he believed that the mysterious whole represented by matter must, necessarily, through resurrection, pass into Heaven. And he looked upon his efforts to further human progress as the necessary condition for the development of a New Earth. Unless he could find a way of doing this he would consider himself to be something less than a man.

So his thinking had moved forward from the crisis in Jersey. What worried him was that it cut clean across the lines of traditionalist Jesuit teaching which always regarded eternal life as the ground of hope. So now he had to set about refining the rough-and-ready formula for which he was groping. And the tools were ready to hand. The test was whether his present circumstances could be shaped by their touch.

Could the war, then, be set within the context of his hopeful evolution? Though he seems to have been shocked by the sheer carnage and destruction of the war Teilhard never seems to have been unduly depressed by it; or, if so, not for long. His friend, Boussac, a fellow geologist, did not share his optimism. One day Teilhard found him gloomy with foreboding, fretting over the social and political upheaval that might follow the ending of the war. So he tried to cheer him by showing him that in fighting he was sharing in progress, and co-operating with the nature for which he had such a profound love. Boussac would have none of this, saying that he did not want to confuse, or even to compare, the brutal doings of generals and the rhetoric of politicians with 'the noble and silent transformation of nature'. Teilhard admitted to his cousin that he often shared Boussac's distaste, or at least understood it, but believed it to be based on an illusion which the right perspective would banish.

Yes, the moral and social development of humanity is indeed the natural and authentic consequence of organic evolution. This development has an ugly look because we see it at too close a range and because free will has its own particular and alluring forms of corruption, but it is in fact the normal term of a process which no doubt is 'noble and silent' simply because we see it from so great a distance – just as shrapnel bursting around an aircraft, seen from a long way off, makes a very pretty picture, purely ornamental in appearance. All moral perversions are found in embryo in the most natural of activities, the most passive (in appearance) in the hands of the first cause; and therein they are tamed but not by-passed, nor surmounted, nor overcome.[5]

Thus Teilhard could be optimistic about the war in the long term, and having participated in it he felt himself to be walking with destiny. From the desolate lunar-like landscape of Verdun, innocent of vegetation and strewn with churned-up rubble, where he had been hiding in shell-holes – often having to turn out a corpse before he could scramble in – he was able to write:

I don't know what sort of monument the country will put up to commemorate the great battle. There is only one that would be appropriate: a great figure of Christ. Only the image of the crucified can sum up, express, and relieve all the horror, and beauty, all the hope and deep mystery in such an avalanche of conflict and sorrows. As I looked at this bitter toil, I felt completely overcome by the thought that I had the honour of standing at one of the two or three spots on which, at this very moment, the whole life of the universe surges and ebbs – places of pain, but it is there that a great future (this I *believe* more and more) is taking place.[6]

Keenly-felt personal loss could only move him momentarily from this optimistic view of the events in which he had taken part. When Boussac was killed he was shattered for a time, because, among other things, he had looked forward to working with him in the future.

At first I thought my reaction would be an embittered rejection of all that I had 'adored'.[7] Instead of working to improve things in the world and extend its conquests (in the spirit you know) would it not be better to abandon to its own suicide this ridiculous world that destroys its own finest products – and then, devoting one's mind entirely to supernatural things, sing a dirge over the ruins of all that here below seems beautiful and precious? . . . But then I pulled myself together. I reflected that God constantly, even when it is a matter of the most saintly undertakings, allows the premature disappearance of the instruments best fitted to achieve his glory. I told myself that man's labour, whatever form it may take, must be essentially tenacious, patient, gentle – and it's by uncomplainingly putting right the disorders and obstacles that a new order is doubtless taking shape and painfully clearing for itself a place in the world, – an order by which the brutal shocks and blind disasters that still bruise and so often crush humanity as it blossoms within the chaotic complex of determinism will be reduced to a minimum. And I told myself that I would continue, should God spare me, to work at the earth's task.[8]

So for Teilhard the war was a necessary part of the earth's organic development. In fact he once described it in a biological metaphor of great graphic power, readily understandable by people who have seen the jerky, black-and-white movies of the First World War and the more sophisticated micro-cinematography of a living cell. 'The million men, with their psychic incandecence and internal energy became for me a great evolutionary fact as biologically real as a gigantic molecule of protein.'[9]

Henri Barbusse, whose novel, *Under Fire*, published in 1916, had projected a grim, realistic picture of men under the pressure of trench-warfare, had had a similar thought. At the end of the story the soldiers are brooding over their fate and destiny, cursing their leaders, the vested interests, those who bury themselves in the past, and the parsons 'who seek to excite you and lull you to sleep with the morphine of their Paradise, so that nothing may change'. Then 'a soldier ventures to add this sentence, though he begins it with a lowered voice: "If the present war has advanced progress by one step its miseries and slaughter will count for little." Between two masses of gloomy cloud a tranquil gleam emerges; and that line of light, so black-edged and beset, brings even so its proof that the sun is there.'

Teilhard had no doubts about the sun being there, but it would be wrong to think that he was untouched by the gloomy cloud. If he had faith in the future it was because it transcended a great deal of the disillusion he shared with the millions of men who emerged from the trenches, wiped the mud from their eyes, and still could not see any evidence of the promised land. They too had been touched by moments of glory, comradeship, and valour; but Teilhard knew that it by no means balanced the debit side of the account: corruption, exploitation, and the degrading waste of life. He had himself lost two brothers, several friends, and many members of his Order. He realized that there was no point in saying that those who had died had gone to ever-lasting bliss, and those who had returned had added a few medals to their bank of merit. He saw that only one thing could justify the agony of the past four years: the fact that the world was palpably a better place. In 1919 he had his doubts. 'Doubt, a fundamental doubt that questions the value of every action, haunts our minds, and its shadow lies heavy on our courage'. He believed in the war. Whilst it was raging he had thrown himself into it with exhilaration, as we have seen. Was this the rude awakening? Evidently shaken by the disillusionment of peace he had once more to set his sights on the Idea. Before he was demobilized it had charged him with the vital energy to walk towards the promised land.

On reflecting upon the war he thought that he could see some positive lessons which it had taught and which everybody should be encouraged to learn. The dominant forces in nature work for good. History shows that whenever the world is thrown into the melting-pot by and large it emerges in better shape. Then it was clear that the war had released a vast amount of psychic energy. In fact it had been a short but conclusive field experiment in which mankind was able to test and measure its evolutionary reserves. There were enough and to spare, sufficient latent strength to complete the work of Spirit on earth. In the war Christ was calling to mankind to raise itself by its own efforts to a higher plane of moral being. 'The youthful envelope of the new humanity could be seen beneath the old husks.'[10] Thus the way ahead was clear. Life could still be beautiful.

It was this kind of thinking which was now finding its

way into articles which Teilhard was beginning to circulate. They were never published in any official journal because they expressed too much confidence in human resources. This is why his superiors had reason to be suspicious of some of the soldier-priest's ideas. They had not yet been worked out in a systematic form but a few 'flashes' from *Cosmic Life* (1916) would have in themselves been sufficient to cause a flurry in the headquarters of his Order, let alone the Holy Office in Rome. From the war onwards, Teilhard was set on a collision course with the church.

If a Christian really understands the inexpressibly wonderful work that is being carried on around him, and by him, in the whole of nature, he cannot fail to see that the excitement and delight aroused in him by 'awakening to the cosmos' can be preserved by him not only in the form they take when transposed to a divine Ideal, but also in the substance of their most material and most earthly objects: to do so he has only to learn to appreciate the value of *sacred evolution* as an instrument of beatification and the eternal hopes it contains.[11]

If the Kingdom of God is to come about, man must win the sovereignty of the earth.[12]

The Incarnation is a making new, a restoration of *all* the universe's forces and powers: Christ is the Centre, the Instrument, the End, of the *whole* of animate and material creation: through him everything is created, sanctified, and vivified.[13]

Christ is the term (end point) of even the natural evolution of living beings; evolution is holy.[14]

To identify the dangerous Huxley and Darwin ideas with anything sacred was enough to scare a cotta off a clergyman. Teilhard was playing with fire. And he knew it, for in the same work we find this innocent and moving prayer:

There is one thing more, Lord, just one thing, but it is the most difficult of all, and, what is worse, it is a thing that you, perhaps, have condemned. It is this: if I am to have a share in your kingdom, I must on no account reject this radiant world in the ecstatic delight of which I opened my eyes.[15]

Everything in Teilhard's religious history had taught him to seek salvation of his soul by looking away from the world. His own deepest instincts were drawing him more and more to the world. The tension must have been intolerable, particularly when he took his final vows. It was at that time that he wrote *The Priest*, which reveals the nucleus of his 'sacred worldliness'.

Since today, Lord, I your priest have neither bread, nor wine, nor altar, I shall spread my hands over the whole universe and take its immensity as the matter of my sacrifice. Is not the infinite circle of things the one final Host that it is your will to transmute. . . . Take up in your hands, Lord, and bless this universe that is destined to sustain and fulfil the plenitude of your being amongst us. Make this universe ready to be united with you: and that this may be so, intensify the magnetism that comes down from your heart to draw to it the dust of which we are made.

When that moment comes, Almighty Father, I shall concentrate in myself all the aspiration that rises up to you from these lower spheres – I shall feel the full force of the yearning that seeks expression in my words – I shall look beyond the white host, and with all the strength of my desire and my prayer, with all my power over every substance and every development, I shall pronounce the words: *Hoc est corpus meum* (This is my body).[16]

The traditional Catholic would construe this as blasphemy. The philosopher would dismiss it as gibberish. The poet might get something from it. But it is essentially an affirmation of hope in the goodness of the created world, which speaks from belief to belief; as John Donne said of the Trinity: 'bones to philosophy, but milk to faith'. And it has about it that passionate certainty which, like all prophecy, entertains no doubts: that the universe is in evolution, with the Cosmic Christ its motive power and goal.

III

Teilhard left the army in 1919 and, after a short interlude in Jersey, returned to Paris where the Sorbonne was putting on special courses for ex-servicemen. He took a degree in natural science; but he was already well beyond the graduate stage, and he went immediately to do research once more under Marcellin Boule at the Paris Museum. The trenches round Rheims had produced a quantity of interesting material which had been collected by a local doctor and handed over to Boule. After doing several digs in the area on his own account, Teilhard examined the collection and made his analysis the subject of his doctoral thesis. This he defended in 1922 and a distinguished jury unhesitatingly awarded him a doctorate with honourable mention, one member, an eminent geologist, predicting for him a spectacular scientific future. Soon he was contributing regularly to *L'Anthroplogie*. Election to learned societies and academic honours followed almost as a matter of course.

At about this time the Abbe Breuil introduced Teilhard to another scientist-priest, the Abbé Gaudefroy, who had been offered the Chair of Geology at the Catholic university, L'Institute Catholique. Gaudefroy, however, was a mineralogist, and suggested that the Chair be divided in order to allow Teilhard to lecture on geology. Teilhard had no particular penchant for teaching. In fact he would much rather have been sent to do field work. But he took the job, and soon was having a remarkable influence on the students, and not only on their academic work. Several of these achieved great eminence in their separate fields and, as it has become fashionable in some quarters to pooh-pooh Teilhard's early scientific work, here is the testimony of one of them, Jean Piveteau (currently Professor of Geology at the Sorbonne):

All the young people were enthusiastic about him. We found in our scientific teaching someone young, dynamic, and open-minded; and we followed his teaching with enthusiasm. I cannot remember without emotion the lessons he gave us when he took us out on field work. We went out with him very often. He was a wonderful man, full of life.

On his ideas, well, he led us a little, and sometimes shocked us, because he was a little too avant-garde for us. We all looked at things in an analytic way, and he saw things in a much wider, more general way. I must admit that at this stage there was a certain resistance to accepting his interpretation of the history of life. However, little by little, this was overcome, not so much because of the high personal regard in which he was held, but because he had a new discipline. Though we did not always look at things his way, by and large, we followed the paths he traced out for us, because we believed they led to true renewal.

In the fields he touched, above all in the palaeontology of mammals, he really revitalized the science in France which, after some brilliant exponents at the beginning of the century, had become rather stale. The Americans and Anglo-Saxons had done a lot of work which was hardly known here, and Teilhard brought these new ideas to us – perhaps he was already thinking along these lines. In any case it can honestly be said that between 1925 and 1930 he was the real leader of the French palaeontological school. He was then wholeheartedly in the field of palaeontology, but there is no doubt that little by little this took second place. He even abandoned science somewhat to perfect his philosophical and religious ideas. Then he left for China and there he had other things on his mind.[17]

China was to be the scene of his most important and most spectacular scientific work, and it was to be the setting of the maturing of his Big Idea: the physical universe evolving with its ultimate destiny built in from the start.

NOTES

1. Cuénot, p. 24ff.
2. Ibid., p. 26.
3. *The Making of a Mind* consists of correspondence between Teilhard and his cousin Marguerite Teilhard-Chambon, who wrote under the pseudonym Claude Aragonnes and who was for many years the headmistress of a girls' school.
4. De Lubac, p. 241.
5. *The Making of a Mind*, p. 111.
6. Ibid., p. 119.
7. Boussac was married to a Jeanne Termier, who may have been the daughter of Pierre Termier, the great geologist who wrote *A la gloire de la terre* and who adopted, in face of difficulty, a saying of Leon Bloy : 'Everything that happens is to be adored.' According to George Barbour it was a slogan Teilhard took to himself in face of hardship and affliction.
8. *The Making of a Mind*, p. 123ff.
9. *Le Coeur de la Matière*.

10. *'Cosmic Life'*, in *Writings in Time of War*, p. 281.
11. Ibid., p. 17.
12. Ibid., p. 62.
13. Ibid., p. 59.
14. Ibid., p. 59.
15. Ibid., p. 53.
16. Ibid., article 'The Priest'.
17. In a private communication.

3 'Brooding Old China'

China was something of a shock. The first impression that it made was depressing. The flat, grey, dusty, endless reaches of North China have that effect on many Western visitors. Teilhard was no exception. He too felt flat and weary. He was only just over forty but he was beginning to feel that his best years were behind him. He lost confidence in himself. There were times when he seemed to be tortured by doubt, indecision, and disproportionate worry over trifles. These were the symptoms of a mind under severe stress. Indeed, he may have already scented the difficulties which were in store for him. The Holy Office, the Roman Church's own MI5, then under the conservative Cardinal Merry del Val, had already in 1920 been busy bringing to heel his two friends, Pierre Charles and Auguste Valensin. At that time he told Valensin that the worst thing that could happen would be for him to be sent away to some far-off land. Probably he had a presentiment that that was already on the cards. In any case, he found the atmosphere menacing, and the terrain of China did not lift his spirit.

But it was not only the geography. The whole state of Chinese life set a living question mark against the truth of his Idea. He saw a civilization in its death-throes. There were no marks of progress. The Chinese were intensely materialistic and utterly insensitive to spiritual values. Confused and dazed by the mass of impressions which crowded in on him, he found it hard to go on believing that this disparate and incoherent world was really a prelude to unification. He told Breuil that Mongolia was a slice of the past, a museum of antique specimens, an empty reservoir.

'Try as I will, I can see no promise of progress, no ferment, no "burgeoning" for mankind tomorrow.' And *tomorrow* came more and more to dominate his thoughts. What counted now was not reconstructing the past, reanimating the fossils; but the future. He came to speak of himself as a pilgrim of the future on the way back from a journey made entirely in the past. That future, he came more and more to believe, would disclose some direction and destination which would give shape to the whole of life and bring together into a harmonious whole the palpably diverse and discrete elements of mankind. But China made him acutely aware that the East represented 'a temptation of the multiple'.

In all respects, then, 1923 – when Teilhard first set foot in China – marked the beginning of another critical phase in the development of his thought. He had been seconded from the Institut Catholique and the Paris Museum to help another Jesuit, Emile Licent, who for ten years had been working on the banks of the Yellow River. Licent's ambition was to found a centre for Christian and scientific training in China. At the same time he hoped to build a museum to house his specimens, and a laboratory for further research. By all accounts he was a pretty tough customer – a northerner from Lille who tended to bullock his way through things. But he had learned some Chinese – a task Teilhard never attempted – and he knew the country intimately. China was riven by civil war and infested by brigands. But Licent was a match for natives, robbers, soldiers and the temperament of the climate. As a scientist his main forte was insects and by the time Teilhard arrived he had a considerable collection. He was at heart a collector, rather careless about classification, and with no gift for synthesis. He was therefore at the opposite pole from Teilhard who frequently hinted that the Licent museum was something of a shambles; and there was a fair amount of tension between the two priests from time to time.

Licent had set up the museum in Tientsin and, whilst catching butterflies and moths, he had come across some important fossil-bearing deposits from Kensu which he sent to the Paris Museum for interpretation. Boule handed them over for examination to Teilhard, who immediately wrote to Licent for more information. Licent replied by inviting Teilhard to go and see for himself. Teilhard went and, in June 1923, the two of them set out on their first joint excursion to the Ordos desert. The auguries were not favourable. The shortest route would have taken them through drought-afflicted country and the territory of brigands who had no affection for Europeans, and had a particular distaste for priests. It was rumoured that if priests were found in this area they were likely to be decapitated and their heads festooned on village walls! Teilhard and Licent therefore armed themselves with rifles and set off by train. When the track ran out they continued by mule caravan.

When they got to the banks of the Shara-Osso-Gol where, under the shadow of the Great Wall gazelles, sheep and horses all grazed together, they started extensive excavations. They employed both Chinese and Mongol labourers. In a couple of weeks they had several hundredweights of carved stone pieces, and had discovered the richest palaeolithic bed then known in China. It contained a quantity of prehistoric tools, crudely but unmistakably sharpened, pointed, and edged. The discovery of these signs of prehistoric human industry was a valuable landmark in Chinese history. Teilhard did not minimize its importance. He was exultant and could not wait to tell Breuil about it. But from his correspondence it becomes clear that the 'other things' alluded to by Piveteau were certainly uppermost in Teilhard's mind. He could not concentrate all his attention on the science of palaeontology. Just as, when he was working in the bone-beds of Sussex he heard the refrain, the call of *Evolution*, so now the concept of *mystical science* began to ring in his ears. 'It is only the science of Christ running through all things that really matters. . . . It seems to me that in a sense the true substance to be consecrated each day is the world's development during that day – the bread symbolizing appropriately what creation succeeds in producing, the wine (blood) what creation causes to be lost in exhaustion and suffering in the course of its effort.'[1]

It was this idea which prompted his *Mass on the World* (originally a *Mass on Things*) regarded by many people as a spiritual classic which will survive even if everything else is forgotten. Certainly it is a moving exposition of the mystic *milieu* in which he saw his scientific work, but it is also an almost manic rhapsody, an exuberant celebration of the certainty of his vision.

> Rich with the sap of the world, I rise up towards the Spirit whose vesture is the magnificence of the material universe but who smiles at me far beyond all victories; and, lost in the mystery of the flesh of God, I cannot tell which is the more radiant bliss: to have found the Word and so be able to achieve the mastery of matter, or to have mastered matter and so be able to attain and submit to the light of God.[2]

These are lofty thoughts and reveal the intoxication which overtook Teilhard when the future beckoned him. But he claimed to have his feet firmly on the ground, because it was what he was *finding in the soil* which was projecting him into the future. The key to the future lay in the physical past. It seems as though he was hauling himself out of despair. Immured in Mongolia, he had seen races on their way to extinction – peoples with no spark of creativity, turbid, vague, materialistic. Nothing had distressed him more than the discovery of only the traces of a vanished world. He looked out over the fields trying to hold on to life as they desperately wrestled with the encroaching sand. Then he heard the ghost of dead Asia whisper, 'Now, my brothers of the West; it is your turn.' He suddenly realized that the light that had been kindled in Asia had passed into other hands and something was emerging, inexorably, from the turmoil. He saw himself as peering over the stern of a ship watching the wake of history, but the receding wake was just as much a proof of movement as the spray washing up from the prow.

From that time he was certain that the only genuine science was that which reveals the *growth* of the universe. 'We must look at (the Far East) at dusk when the sun, bearing the spoils of Asia with it in its glory, rises in triumph over the skies of Europe.'[3]

Teilhard still looked upon Europe – and notably Paris – as the intellectual inspiration of his mind, and the axis of progress. From Tienstin, where he had nobody with whom he could share his new ideas, Paris must have seemed a Golden Age away. But soon he discovered that Pekin, the centre of Chinese intellectual life, was also the base from which a large number of foreign scientific missions were working, in particular Swedish and American. He found the contacts he was able to make with the members of such missions greatly to his liking though, at this stage, he was never able to be with them for very long. Moreover, he found also in Pekin several Chinese geologists in whom he detected a fellow feeling for the good Earth. Although the Idea was never far from his mind, the greater part of his time was devoted to examining and reporting on the geological strata and the fossils which he had gathered on the two excursions which followed his fruitful investigation of the Ordos. The monographs which he published in the journals during this period indicate an enormous capacity for work. Most of them were devoted to purely technical matters: *The Geology of Northern Chihli and Eastern Mongolia, Cenozoic Vertebrate Fossils of East Kansu, Notes on the Structure of Mountains to the West of Linnmingkwan*, and papers of that sort. But here and there we detect a speculative note: *The Law of Irreversibility in Evolution*, for instance. And we know that to his trusted friends he was circulating typescript copies of much bolder thinking: *Pantheism and Christianity*, and *My Universe* were among them. This kind of thinking needed a much wider and more liberal culture than even Pekin could provide. He needed the company and stimulus of a multitude of different minds. He needed libraries, laboratories, and all the other things

55

which Paris could offer him. So he made one last excursion, a sad pilgrimage to Shanghai to see his sister's grave – and then, in the autumn of 1924, Teilhard returned to France reflecting that the year's retreat had done him good, and relishing the prospect of a milieu where he could discuss and preach the things which lay closest to his heart. 'I have an impression that the earth, whilst retaining its prodigious power of communicating the divine to us through all its being, is becoming paler and paler to me as regards its present and its past. It is the future that is fascinating, and I see it all ablaze with God springing up everywhere.'[4]

The quotation is from a letter written to Leontine Zanta.

Leontine Zanta was a woman: and this is perhaps the place to say something about Teilhard and women. They were necessary to him. Some of the books hint mysteriously at 'a crisis of sexuality'. Friends say he 'had to be careful with women'. In his last spiritual testament he wrote,

There would be an essential element missing from this story of my interior vision . . . if I did not mention in closing that, from the critical moment when, rejecting the old moulds of family and religion, I began to awaken and really to express myself, nothing developed in me which was not under a woman's gaze or a woman's influence. Here, nothing more will be expected of me than general, half-adoring homage rising from the depths of my being towards those women whose warmth and charm have, drop by drop, passed into the bloodstream of my dearest ideas.[5]

Now Teilhard did not meet women 'in the flesh' until he was thirty. Up to then he had been too preoccupied with the impersonal. But when he found himself smitten, all sorts of spiritual energies were released. Having reflected on its meaning, he brought *the experience* into the service of the Idea. He realized that man could not be brought to maturity without a sentimental influence to sensitize his intelligence. (*Le feminin* (or the unitive) was as essential as oxygen or vitamins.) But he seems to have been very confused about the positive role that sexuality may play. He conceives of marriage as focusing on reproduction, and chastity as mutual

56

attraction sublimated. There seems to be no middle way. In a slightly amusing passage he laments that copulating couples dissipate a lot of energy that could quite well have been put to other uses – research, for instance! 'Let us look very coolly as biologists or engineers at the lurid atmosphere of our great towns at evening. There, and everywhere else as well, the earth is continually dissipating its most marvellous power. . . . How much energy do you think the spirit of the earth loses in a single night ?'[6] Teilhard had discovered the spiritual qualities inherent in a sentimental-platonic relationship and he has important things to say about 'the couple'. He admits to its positive value but sees the danger of their love becoming an end in itself and therefore demonic. In suggesting that erotic love should be sublimated into mental energy, he sounds like a manichean; unaware that the rhapsody of bodies may achieve not sublimation but *the sublime*, in which creative energies, directed initially towards the other, are transmuted in the act, and radiate in all directions.

In any event, it is clear from his life, as it is from his confession, that a succession of women played an important part in 'drawing him on'. (Das Ewig-Weibliche zieht uns an – the eternal feminine draws us on.) Amongst these Leontine Zanta had her own important place. She was a woman of charm and great intellectual energy – the first Frenchwoman to become a doctor of philosophy. She was a celebrated feminist and held regular salons where some of the most original thinkers of the day could test each other's ideas. Bergson was a frequent visitor; and so was Teilhard. Now that his mind was developing simultaneously on several different levels he needed the stimulus of a variety of thinkers. Breuil and Boule struck scientific sparks; Auguste Valensin and Pierre Charles, Jesuit comrades from Jersey days, served as theological foils. But he needed to check and develop his thought with the help of someone with a wide range of knowledge and a sharp intelligence. Such a man was Edouard Le Roy, the mathematician and philosopher.

Le Roy was only ten years older than Teilhard, but Teilhard looked upon him as a father and was constantly grateful to him, particularly for the way in which he had fostered loyalty to the church. The two men met each Wednesday evening and Teilhard was able to lay bare much of the heterodox thinking that had necessarily remained unexpressed whilst he was abroad. On many matters the two men found themselves very near to each other, so much so that years afterwards neither of them could remember who had thought of what first. One of the advantages of the relationship was that Le Roy could incorporate some of Teilhard's radical ideas into the lectures he was giving at the College de France without drawing too much attention to them. (Though, some time later, Le Roy found himself on the Index!)

Both men saw the capital importance of finding new modes of describing the way things have come to be as they are. In other words, they called for a fresh phenomenology. This in its turn demanded new words (neologisms) to describe fresh categories. Teilhard was not content with describing the physical layers of earth: the lithosphere, the atmosphere, and so on. Another scientist (Edouard Suess) had coined the word *biosphere* to describe the 'layer' of living things which had no power of reflection: plants, animals, and so on. Teilhard saw other layers: a *thinking layer* consisting in mankind, its interrelatedness, technology, culture and spiritual values. This he called *noosphere* and the long process which brought it to birth he called *noogenesis*. And for the most important part of this process – the making of upright, thinking, reflective Man – he used the word *hominisation*.

These words are admittedly difficult, especially for people who cannot guess their meaning from the Greek roots; but they are nothing more than the shorthand in which Teilhard noted down the causal relationships which he thought he could see between things. To see and make others see was what, above all, he wanted to do. His phenomenology was not an academic exercise. At heart it was evangelical. He wanted to increase people's capacity to live. 'To see or to perish.' And to this task he set himself when he returned to his bench in the Paris Museum and his classroom at the Institut Catholique.

He found himself in great demand. His short absence had turned him into something of a legend amongst the new students at the Institut, the Sorbonne, the Polytechnique, and the Ecole Normale Supérieure. They responded enthusiastically to his ideas, for he appeared to be breaking down the barrier between the sacred and the profane. They glimpsed the outlines of a sanctity which made their secular vocations holy and gave impetus and direction to their necessary preoccupation with the world of things. 'Work in the world was presented to us', said one of them, 'as the most immediate realization of God's will, the extension of his most central designs for the world.'[7]

This may seem pretty old hat to us now, but in the context of the rigid Catholicism of France half a century ago it must have come like a revelation from on high. It was not surprising, then, that the students wanted from 'the long thin priest' more than the sanctification of their studies. They wanted to know whether he could blow some of the cobwebs from the fusty old doctrines which for so long had been a hindrance to an intelligent acceptance of the faith. Teilhard relished such encounters but sometimes got carried away whilst 'thinking on his feet', scaring even some of his closest comrades. There was one occasion when he allowed himself to be drawn on the question of original sin and, as his answers got progressively less and less orthodox, a friend had to take him by the elbow and gradually edge him towards the door!

Many of his privately-circulated notes treated of original sin. Some of them turned up in Rome. How they got there is a mystery. They were probably stolen from his desk in the Institut. But they threw the Holy Office into a frenzy. Teilhard had scarcely settled in France when he was summoned to the Superior of his Order in Lyons to explain his position.

The Holy Office was quite right to be disturbed by some of Teilhard's ideas. If, in fact, despite a few blind-alleys and dead-ends, the world was *necessarily* evolving towards its proper and divinely appointed end, a great deal of orthodox doctrine was put at risk, and none more so than that related to man's freedom and sin. Conversely, the traditional interpretation of original sin as a historical catastrophe posed a profound problem for Teilhard's optimistic view of human nature.

Now Teilhard was not a good biblical theologian. In fact most of his biblical knowledge seems to derive from liturgy, and he admitted to a young Anglican laywoman that she knew far more of the Bible than he did. We can only guess at the kind of interpretation he had been taught of the first few chapters of the Book of Genesis. Teilhard was right to reject it as history, but he had not the necessary knowledge to interpret it in a way more in keeping with newer ideas of biblical criticism and human psychology. No doubt if, as a geologist, he had excavated in the Middle East a fossilized apple with a couple of bites in it, he would have been a candidate for beatification! As it was, in turning away from the story of Adam and Eve and interpreting original sin in terms of what he thought he was able to see, he was hell bent for the Index. Both Charles and Valensin had encouraged him to do some experimental thinking on the subject, but his notes were tentative and provisional – Aunt Sallys which he had put up for criticism and discussion among those close to him. But they were too much for the Holy Office. Teilhard was asked to sign a document stating that he would never again write or say anything against the traditional position of the church on original sin.

The affair dragged on for some time. The Principal of the Institut and his immediate superiors were on his side. But Rome was intractable. He had to sign the document. He was ordered not to teach at the Institut, and to leave Paris.

So he returned to China – an exile. At the time he did not realize the full consequences of pulling up his roots from 'the incomparable milieu of that warm and wonderful Paris'. He tried to put a good face on it, but inwardly he was in torment. It would have been easy enough to contract out of the church for good and all. One or two people advised him to. But that line of action was in conflict with his deepest convictions. He really believed, in spite of his 'sacred aversion to ecclesiasticism' that the Roman Catholic Church was the guardian of the Truth. (What he thought about other churches was another matter!) And the whole point of his life was that his Idea could be contained and expressed within the life of the church. If he abandoned the church it would be tantamount to saying that he was wrong. His clear duty therefore was to stay. But from this point his life was lived inside a web of difficulties which officialdom spun round him. But for the time being the crisis of obedience was over. He decided to go forward with a 'shameless optimism'. 'If there is a God, as I believe, he will make the obstacle serve my progress; and in the end I will find myself more able than ever to make the light shine which some would like to see extinguished. . . . What I greatly desire to propagate is not exactly a theory, a system, a *Weltanschauung*, but a certain taste, a certain perception of beauty, the pathos, and the unity of *being*.'[8]

This clearly shows the mystical side of Teilhard's mind, and the intuitive 'taste' which allowed him to find in China, as previously he had found in Flanders, the food he needed to nourish his spirit. He began to see China with new eyes – as 'unrisen dough' which, once awakened, would become a formidable force. He had confidently predicted that the Reds were going to win the battle for the minds of the Chinese. He was soon writing: 'There is going on here at this very moment a human development of almost geological dimensions; to participate in it would be a rare chance indeed.'

Teilhard's detractors might be inclined to say that from

this point on a note of messianism can be heard in his voice. 'Messianism' is no doubt too harsh a word to use, but there are clear signs that Teilhard believed himself to possess a unique vision about the unfolding of the universe and the essentially Christian basis of its movement. He even regarded himself as a 'Knight Errant', hoping to gain a bit of notoriety, and thus achieving the power to make himself heard. He wanted a public platform from which to expound to all men the truth which was struggling to emerge from the depth of his being: *the World in Me*. It is impossible to overestimate the emotional and mental energy which the discovery of this idea brought to him. Teilhard was a new man *in the world*, just as there have been new men *in Christ*, and new men *in Marx* – men who have been possessed by what Jung described as a master-principle which draws together and interprets all other phenomena and makes them *tick*. 'What is truth,' said Søren Kierkegaard, 'but to live for the Idea.'

Teilhard knew that he had been given the Idea and he wanted to proclaim it from the house-tops. But from China nobody would hear. So he had to return to the written word. Even then he was trapped. He wanted earnestly to speak of the Idea as it emerged from the specificity of China, but he had neither the language nor the knowledge which would serve as a key to the hidden treasure; nor had he – and this is important for an understanding of Teilhard's way of arriving at truth – 'the magical *intuition* that would enable me to perceive the secret beauty *instinctively and more surely than any science*'.[9]

Teilhard wanted passionately to be free to speak without the muzzle of dogmatic presuppositions or accepted ideas. He wanted to reveal the *primary quality of being* to which he had penetrated beneath the secondary qualities of race, nationality, coterie, and sect. The text he would have taken not from holy scripture, but from Paul Morand, *Nothing but the Earth* – four words he rated as being worth far more than a whole book. Although Teilhard kept talking about *matter being spiritualized in us*, the expression 'nothing but the earth' smacks of materialism. It is therefore proper to ask whether the political corollaries of such a positivistic attitude to the world did not follow. They did. Teilhard despised the 'egoistical proportions of almost all present social institutions' and realized that to be logical he had to call for their liquidation. Having seen man as a phenomenon – an extension of geology where classes and groupings other than purely scientific ones are irrelevant – he realized that human continuity can be carried forward only by tearing down all kinds of old walls.

Three things, however, prevented Teilhard from turning Marxist. Constitutionally he was not the stuff of which revolutionaries are made; he was a soft, gentle and charming man, courteous and self-effacing; he was also a scientist, preoccupied with pure theories and innocent of the brutal realities of the tough political world – though he realized nearly fifty years ago that the very 'meagreness of the (earthly) domain' would necessitate some sort of radical and dramatic action. Thirdly, he was prevented from becoming a revolutionary by the clerical collar. Much of the church's teaching turned his dog-collar into a yoke and, as we have seen, he was as impatient of this as he was of the obsolete structures and institutions which were preventing man building the earth. But the church's scriptures spoke of a Cosmic Christ, and Teilhard latched on to this doctrine with enthusiasm. He seems to have been somewhat disinterested in the Incarnation as such – the earthly life of Jesus – and refers to it only occasionally, saying indeed on one occasion that he had a distaste for that evangelism which centres on the human and moral qualities of Jesus. He had simply no need for Jesus as a friend, or brother, or companion in life's way. (The Holy Office had a point here, when they heard a priest under-valuing the critical and decisive earthly ministry of Jesus.) What he required was a Force as vast and as real as Matter itself – a Force capable of evoking adoration, with a numinous quality of greater power than the *kitsch* models and plaques which had projected the image of Jesus in home and school. He wanted SOMEONE to be the Universe. Such a Force he found only in the Christ of St John and St Paul – and in particular in the Epistle to the Colossians. Here, in his view, Christ was presented to man as the true Soul of the World. Only in such a presence could he love him.

Thus one of the perversely difficult parts of the New Testament was instrumental in saving Teilhard for the church. He did not use the concept of the Cosmic Christ to give theological verisimilitude to an otherwise positivistic-looking theory. He may, indeed he did, expound the idea in a way which was quite original, and in language which certainly would have caused many a curial eyebrow to twitch; but there can be little doubt that he thought that he was elaborating a doctrine which revelation had given to the church. He began to use it in the 'spiritual book' to which at this time his letters sometimes refer, *The Divine Milieu*. During his service with the army he had thought that he could detect a universal soul struggling to be born. (He described it as a wraith.) Its mysterious quality consisted in its being partly a human creation, yet indubitably Other, entering into communion with us and yet having the full force of Absolute Being. This Being concentrated on a single point, a single Person: Jesus. Now Teilhard saw this same Jesus as the mighty, majestic Creator of all, the Pantocrator of the Byzantine mosaics. 'Nothing less than this Parousia is needed to counterbalance and dominate in our hearts the glory of the world that is coming into view. And so (Lord) that we may triumph over the world with you, come to us clothed *in the glory of the world*.'[10] Thus when Teilhard speaks of 'the World in Me' he is at the same time saying 'the Christ in me', but the Christ is immeasurably larger than the flaxen-haired young curate image which contemporary Christian iconography, both Protestant and Catholic, was then projecting. When, years later, Teilhard re-read *The Divine Milieu*, he was astonished to find how the essential features of his vision had been fixed at this time.

This christo-cosmic vision represented by 'the world in me' meant that in Teilhard's mind heaven and earth were in a state of continuous dialogue and synthesis. His busy-ness with the earth increased in tempo as specimens were discovered, identified, and described. His bibliography for this period alone runs to ten pages. By now he was established as a scientist with a considerable reputation, and he found himself more and more in demand at the Pekin Headquarters of The National Geological Survey for China, the base for some of the most distinguished geologists and anthropologists of the day, like Davidson Black and Sven Hedin. In time the Carnegie Foundation appointed him to be one of the Survey's directors.

In this capacity he assumed direction of some excavations at Chou-kou-tien, a village on the edge of the western hills not far from Pekin. A preliminary examination had suggested to him that the site might be a rich field of investigation. The idea that primitive man lay buried thereabouts had first been mooted in 1918, when a Swedish prospector had come across some pieces of chipped white-vein quartz in a limestone quarry. But, though the site had been excavated in 1922, in the intervening years scarcely any other evidence of the presence of early man had been detected. When Teilhard took charge in 1929, an early winter set in, so he ordered digging to stop, and the site to be closed down until the spring. Dr Pei, a young Chinese geologist, paid off the coolies and, before returning to Pekin, went back to take the measurements of the hole so that they could be included in his report. Whilst probing the sand with his measuring-stick he uncovered the smooth dome of a skull. He dislodged it carefully and when it was free of the rock he realized that the top of the cranium was bigger than that of any known ape. He took it to his room and spent the night making photographs, buying up the local shop's supply of candles. The next morning he hired a rickshaw to take him the thirty-five miles to Pekin and rode with the skull safely hidden under his scholar's robe. By nightfall he had delivered it to Davidson Black, who began to work on the restoration with dental tools. He worked ceaselessly for some days, never leaving his task until the early hours of the morning when he placed the skull in a strong-box. Black realized that he had a very important find on his hands, and was convinced that the specimen was human; but before announcing it he got Teilhard to confirm his judgment by establishing the geological period in which the cave had been in use. This was how Sinanthropus (or Pekin Man), the precursor of Homo Sapiens in China, first saw the light of day. Some reliable books, like *Petit Larousse*, proclaim Teilhard as its discoverer, but he never made such a claim himself, and it always pained him when he got the credit for it.

He had, however, played an important role by his accurate identification of the rock layers and, some years later, his uncanny intuition again paid off. He advised the drilling of a horizontal gully and a vertical shaft on the same site. This revealed a cave in which were found animal bones, neolithic skulls, primitive tools, a bone needle and a tooth-necklace. There were dog-faced baboons, Sinanthropus, and Homo Sapiens – all in the same hole. No wonder Teilhard exclaimed, 'What a hotel!' He described Pekin Man as 'a being in whom the fire of thought was already alight and had been for some time – already Homo Faber (tool-making), walking upright, and using his hands as we do.' Pekin Man turned out to be a woman and Teilhard nick-named her 'Nelly'.[11] The finding of Nelly was further evidence that human beings were a product of evolutionary change, but it did nothing to undermine Teilhard's conviction that man was essentially a spiritual being.

III

The experience of Chou-kou-tien whetted Teilhard's appetite for more team-work and he increasingly found himself on projects with international groups. In 1930 he joined the

Chapman Andrews expedition into the Gobi desert. This was covered by *The National Geographical Magazine* and from the photographs and a small amount of cine film we get a good picture of what Teilhard looked like in the field. He was a slim, athletic figure, dressed in breeches, heavy boots, an army shirt, and a battered old trilby! His movements were quick and precise as he chipped away at the rock in an attempt to get to know the structural relationship between China and Mongolia. But evidently his mind was being extended to other horizons, for his interests were gradually shifting from the material and organic layers of the earth to 'the thinking layer which man constitutes on our planet. . . . Once a person has grasped, through the study of rocks and bones, the scale of organicity of the human milieu in which we are plunged, he discovers a magnificent object of study.'[12]

The following year he was invited to be the geologist on the famous 'Yellow Expedition' or *Croisière Jaune* which the Citroën Motor Company organized to test their vehicles over the old silk routes of China. The track lay over some of the most difficult terrain in the world. It was to last almost a whole year and promised to be a strenuous time, even for young men. Teilhard was now fifty and wondered whether he could stand up to such rigorous conditions, but he joined in high spirits and, for the second time in his life, he found himself rubbing shoulders with men of a very different background from his own: tough, materialist mechanics and engineers who when photographed together looked like an international rugby team.

Teilhard did his best to fit in with them but, as time went on and the expedition was hampered by delays (caused as much by obdurate Chinese governors and by brigands as by mechanical failure) he began to notice a great gap which separated him, fundamentally, from the hearty men who surrounded him. Though he could chat to them easily enough about this and that, he found it difficult to communicate to them some of his deepest and most passionate beliefs. It is, of course, amusing to imagine him explaining the mystical and incandescent qualities of rock to a mechanic who is trying to dislodge a boulder that has just wrenched the caterpillar-track from the wheels! But he soon was able to put his finger on the real difficulty of communication. It was not that the men had no experience of the Christian faith, or had lost touch with it. It was that they were thinking and functioning in a totally different milieu from his own. They were engineers immured in a world of things and functions. So it was not just a question of finding a new language into which he could translate his ideas; but of finding a new myth which centred religious activity in the world of concrete things; that is, in the organicity of the human milieu. 'In future, faith in Christ will never hold its own, or be extended, except through the intermediary of faith in the world.'

On New Year's Day the expedition reached a Christian Mission and Teilhard tried hard to find something to say which would be meaningful to his tough, agnostic colleagues.

My friends, we have met in this little church in the heart of China to come before God at the beginning of this New Year. No doubt each of us sees God in a different way. Yet, because we are intelligent beings, not one of us can escape the feeling that there exists above and beyond ourselves some superior force, who therefore possesses some superior form of our own intelligence and will. What we ask of this enveloping, universal Presence is that it may reunite us, as through a common living centre, with those we love, who are beginning this New Year so far away from us. So may joy dwell in our hearts, and all around us; and may success crown our enterprise.[18]

When it was over Teilhard did rate the enterprise a success, for though the conditions were hardly ideal for the patient sifting of evidence and specimens which was the basis of his research, it had provided him with an understanding of the geology of Central Asia which he described as 'a revelation'. 'For that, ten months of my life, even at the age of fifty, is not too much to pay.'

IV

Every so often Teilhard was allowed to return to France for a short period. He visited his family and friends, spent a great deal of time in libraries bringing himself up to date, and sharpened his wits in the company of other scholars. During one such leave a mysterious fever laid him low and all his plans went by the board. In the enforced period of idleness he had time to reflect on the stage of life at which he had arrived. Two things became clear. One emerged from contemplating the evolution of his own interior life; not, as might be expected, the value of God's love in the making of his soul, but 'the astounding value and function of the love of God in *the building of the world*.' He began to see that the love of *God* is the highest form of *human* energy, and that Christianity is a new phylum, that is, a new kind of organism, in the natural world. After his recovery he left Marseilles for Shanghai, and during the voyage he developed this theme in *Human Energy*, one of his more important essays. At this time the 'vast collectivities' of Nazism and Fascism were making a total claim on the energy of humanity and centring it on themselves, that is on the collectivity. Teilhard, who tended to be impressed by any movement that was organizing change, saw that because they did not ultimately centre on a *Someone*, Fascism and Nazism were doomed, and that in their systems the personal was at risk. He also saw Christians as having a personal centre but no effective 'sphere' (organization), and wished that the 'centre without the sphere' and the 'sphere without the centre' could come together so that the totalitarian movements could 'succeed in taking soul and personality by drawing near to God whom they seem about to abolish'.[14] This shows how little Teilhard understood the nature of the romantic vitalities which were breaking out in Nazism and, though the essay is a deeply moving exposition of human energy when it centres on God, it suggests a naïve view of the power residing on 'the dark side' of human personality, especially when it manifests itself in collective forms.

The second thing brought home to Teilhard during his illness was that the days of active work in the field were now almost over. So he snatched the chance, whenever he could, of seeing the rest of Asia. He made a 'whistle stop tour' – in a geologist's view of time! – of India, South China, Burma and Java. On several of these excursions he was accompanied by a brilliant German geologist, Helmut de Terra, whose book[15] describes him at this time as being 'full of his theories of a universe converging on Christ'. 'His scientific work gave the impression that he had already formulated his ideas and was only waiting for external observation to prove them well founded. His vision of a common destiny had become such a mission with him that the new scientific data had to take second place.' De Terra's book gives a remarkable and perceptive account of Teilhard's personality, of the roots of his serenity, and the happiness he found in research. Though he was critical of Teilhard's impatience of environmental factors in the story of evolution, never once does he infer that Teilhard's work was unscientific. He knew that over-concentration on too narrow a field places a severe restriction on the understanding of man's place in nature. He also accepted the basically religious nature of man's quest for knowledge and urge for research, quoting in support the greatest scientist of the age, Albert Einstein:

> . . . science can only be created by those who are thoroughly imbued with the aspiration towards truth and understanding. This source of feeling, however, springs from the sphere of religion. . . . The situation may be expressed by an image: science without religion is lame, religion without science is blind.[16]

NOTES

1. *Letters from a Traveller*, p. 86.
2. *Hymn of the Universe*, p. 27.
3. *Letters from a Traveller*, p. 103.
4. *Letters to Leontine Zanta*, pp. 65ff.
5. *Le Coeur de la Matière*.
6. *Human Energy*, pp. 32ff.
7. Cuénot, p. 60.

8. *Letters to Two Friends*, p. 58.
9. Ibid., p. 44, italics mine.
10. *Le Milieu Divin*, p. 128, italics mine.
11. Cuénot, pp. 172ff.
12. Ibid., p. 120.
13. Ibid., p. 133.
14. *Human Energy*, pp. 158ff.
15. *Memories of Teilhard de Chardin*, Collins 1964.
16. *Out of My Later Years*, Thames & Hudson 1950, p. 29.

4 'We are Evolution'

Teilhard now set out to make the lame to leap and the blind to see. The outbreak of the Sino–Japanese war helped. Excavation was slowed down. Collections were dispersed. Colleagues did not return from Europe. Funds dried up. Teilhard, unable to travel, unexpectedly found himself with time for reflection and was able to develop his Big Idea in the long-contemplated book about man. This was to be an exposition of his vision of man's place in the universe. It was to be entirely independent of speculation and dogma, dealing solely with man as an observable 'thing': *The Phenomenon of Man*. It is the only book of any length which Teilhard wrote. All the other 'works' are collections of essays written at different times and frequently repetitive. From these it is possible to piece together a rough and often personal picture of his world-view. In *The Phenomenon of Man* he expounds it in a logical, direct, and quite impersonal way.

Now though it is true that Teilhard assures us that his phenomenology is based on an empirical investigation of data ('photographable' was how he described it), it would be quite wrong to think that other factors were not informing his intelligence. We have already seen how some of his closest friends hinted that 'other things' occasionally made him impatient of some scientific facts. And it is quite wrong, it seems to me, to disregard his existential situation, as some writers tend to when they say that Teilhard's vision did not spring from an inner agony. Certainly we do not come across anything approximating to the weepings of Augustine's *Confessions*, the anxious introspection of Kierkegaard's

Journals, or the mortification of Pascal's *Pensées*. But Teilhard plainly had an obsession. It was what he later called 'the death barrier'. Over fifty years separate the small boy, turning in terror from his combustible hair, and this passage from *The Phenomenon of Man:*

> If an isolated man can imagine that it is possible, physically, or even morally, for him to contemplate a complete suppression of himself – confronted with total annihilation (or even simply with an insufficient preservation) destined for the fruit of his evolutionary labour – mankind, in its turn, is beginning to realize for once and for all that its only course would be to go on strike. For the effort to push the earth forward is much too heavy, and the task threatens to go on much too long, for us to continue to accept it, unless we are to work in what is incorruptible.[1]

To say that this is a more sophisticated version of the child's ultimate concern is not to say that Teilhard is projecting into his work a neurosis of childhood. (And even if he were he would be in good company. There is a touch of psychopathology in the work of many creative thinkers. Freud, Darwin, Marx, and Simone Weil would be among his companions.) But undeniably the death-barrier was of vital and deep personal concern.

Factors other than naked evidence were subtly shaping his mind. Teilhard was no philosopher. (Certainly a philosophy of sorts is inherent in his writings. But he did not know much about philosophical method. He seems to have been unaware of the main elements of twentieth-century philosophy. Probably he never made a systematic study of Freud or Marx. It was this that lay behind Etienne Gilson's catty comment, 'I see what he believes; but what does he know?') But during his theological training a certain amount of scholastic philosophy had brushed off on him. Bits of his system have a resonance of the Fathers. Take Augustine, for instance. In *The City of God* he claims that every separate part is conscious of a possible greater unity. 'Every beginning looks towards some end, proper to its own genus, and every part looks towards that whole, regarded as a whole, of which it is a part.'[2] In Teilhard this quality forms part of what he calls the 'within' of things. Augustine conceives of peace as the harmonious working together of many different parts, so creating a greater order. This kind of 'complexity' is fundamental to Teilhard. In Book 19 of *The City of God* Augustine detects an 'urge' in inanimate things which brings about change and makes order to appear out of disorder. The 'urge' gives man and nature their function – the realization of their potentialities, implying some kind of direction and purpose. This is nearly what Teilhard means by 'psychic energy'. In Book 22 Augustine speaks of a metamorphosis of earthly bodies into heavenly bodies, which looks as though he has anticipated by some fifteen hundred years Teilhard's views of the mechanism of the Millennium!

Teilhard does not speak much about Blaise Pascal, but he was clearly familiar with the *Pensées*. To some extent both of them start from the same place: man, part of nature, and dying nature, but at least *conscious* that he is dying, and therefore greater than nature, poised perilously 'between the nothing and the all'. Pascal spoke of three orders of being: Body, Thought, Charity; Teilhard of Biosphere, Noosphere, Love (Omega). Both men were steeped in scientific phenomena. Pascal found them cold and repelling. Turning to religion, he proclaimed a tragic vision of the world. Teilhard, on the other hand, turned more and more to science because in it he found his optimistic vision of the future.

Teilhard was no more a theologian than he was a philosopher. A theology of sorts is inherent in his system, just as it is in the works of Shakespeare, but that does not make him a theologian. He did not know the Bible well. He seems to have gleaned little information about the critical controversies of his day. As we have seen, he claimed to have great affection for St Paul and St John but, unless he was deliberately censoring the passages which did not fit into his scheme, his knowledge of them was neither profound nor comprehensive.

This does not add up to what Peter Medawar called 'a deliberate willingness to be deceived'; but it does indicate an unconscious tendency to turn a Nelson's eye to those theological facts which signalled defeat for his Idea.

Something must also be said about the difficulty of Teilhard's language. Very often he uses words with extraordinary precision; but he also uses metaphorical expressions drawn from a wide area. The reader has to be something of a polymath, and metaphor and allegory are notoriously difficult for precise expression. It is therefore sometimes hard to pin him down. This is because he himself was groping around for precise concepts, and his language is an approximation to the truth of what he saw. The visionary was never far away. He was struggling to reveal that which he thought he saw, but which no man had ever seen in quite this way. It was in some respects an essentially private vision, like that of Blake, who could see 'a world in a grain of sand' but, like Dante, he struggled to reveal it in an ordered and logical way. Like Dante, too, he had to invent a new language and a new myth. The reader has thus often to reach for the meaning behind the language. We saw how, in 1914, he likened *the million men* to a gigantic molecule of protein – a powerful and gripping image. But he went on to describe their *psychic incandescence*. This is more difficult; the two words are never found in this juxtaposition; they are drawn from different disciplines. It is like talking about *rhombic neurosis*. But to Teilhard *psychic incandescence* was virtually a visual quality. It is, however, only when you understand in general terms what he means by *human energy* that the troops begin to glow! You can see what he was getting at, but he is using language outside the meaning of the act. But this should not deter us, any more than inadequacies in Teilhard's theology or knowledge of history should deter us, from coming to terms with the basic outline of his Idea.

The key is *Time*. As Augustine said, we all know what it is until we have to define it. It is something which chops up our existence into years and days. It is something in the hinterland of our life. But, as a geologist and palaeontologist, Teilhard had to have it in the forefront of his mind. It is impossible to think about rock and fossils without thinking about *duration*, and he soon came to see that it is just as impossible to describe a thing outside the context of what preceded and followed it, as it is to describe the setting of something in space without relating it to what is beside it. But time marches on. So everything that is has its place in a *process of becoming*. It is part of an irreversible movement. You cannot put the clock back, and if you string things in order along the line of time, no thing can change place with any other thing. That would make for an absurd sequence, like infancy, middle-age, youth, childhood. Thus, all things are in process of *becoming*. The world is still in the process of being born – what Teilhard called *cosmogenesis*. Man is both actor and spectator of this process, and being part of it, he is therefore unfinished.

Now evolution, to give *cosmogenesis* its more usual name, is not just an interesting sidelight thrown on to human destiny. It is the most important factor in our environment. All experience must be seen in its light. It is so fundamental to our life that it virtually acts as a fourth dimension. 'Evolution is a light illuminating all facts, a curve which all lines must follow.' It is therefore *vitally* important to remember that our world is going somewhere. There is direction. Teilhard envisaged an end-point to this development and he called it *Omega*, and, though he was digging up the past, for him the future point on which evolution converged was just as important as looking back towards the *Alpha* of our origins. In other works, life must be judged not from the point of view of the slime from which man has emerged, but from the greatness to which he may aspire. It is the oak tree which gives the acorn its significance.

But, he argues, there is a necessary connection between protoplasm and Christ, for it is fundamental to Teilhard's thought that nothing can evolve which is not already present in the most primitive stuff of the universe. So Alpha and Omega are not strangers.

The way from Alpha to Omega is marked by sign-posts showing where things took a critical leap forward and where boundaries into new kinds of being were crossed. The key to the map was found in Teilhard's own subject. Look, he seems to say, look at all those dull bits of rock and fossil which most people hasten by when they visit a museum. They are far more important to my argument than the products of historical time: spinning-wheels, sedan-chairs, and all that sort of thing. When you put rocks and fossils in order along the scale of time, you will find beyond doubt that things have been on the move, are still moving, and are equipped to go further. The time-scale is pretty long – some three hundred million years – and if you examine the fossils at intervals of, say, a hundred thousand years, you will find the differences in them scarcely perceptible. But if you observe the start and end of a span of ten million years, you will find that 'life has practically grown a new skin'.

Change, of course, does not necessarily mean progress, but it is impossible to deny that, with the passage of time, matter organizes itself into more complicated forms. There is a distinct inclination towards organisms with more sensitive and elaborate nervous systems. In fact, it would be possible to mark time not by ticking off aeons, but by observing the stage of complexification at which organisms had arrived. Thus life can be seen to move, and to move in a certain direction: towards more complexity. Even more, Teilhard would argue, along with the intensification and complexification of nervous tissues, there also develops an increasing *consciousness*. Some animals clearly have a mind of sorts which did not arrive by divine fiat. It developed. So consciousness, or its possibility, must be present in material systems. A 'rising tide of consciousness visibly manifests itself . . . in the course of the ages'. This phenomenon became Teilhard's *Law of Complexity Consciousness*, probably his greatest contribution to phenomenology. It is a law which 'sacred evolution' offers from the fossil beds; but it is dependent on a function which you can observe in all things, on whichever side of the fossils you look, either before life appeared, or in historical time: a built-in capacity to unite. The flow of life 'above and ahead' could not have taken place without this technique. So the highest quality of man's life, the capacity to love, what Teilhard calls *amorsiation*, really depends on the ability of the most rudimentary forms to get together.

> Love . . . is a general property of all forms of life. . . . In mammals, so close to ourselves, it is easily recognized. . . . Lower down on the tree of life, analogies are more obscure until they become so faint as to be imperceptible. But this is the place to repeat what I said earlier, when we were discussing the 'within' of things. If there were no internal propensity to unite, even at a prodigiously rudimentary level – indeed the molecule itself – it would be physically impossible for love to appear higher up, with us, in 'hominised' form . . . We should assume its presence, at least in an inchoate form, in everything that is. . . . Driven by the forces of love, the fragments of the world seek each other so that the world may come into being. This is no metaphor; and it is much more than poetry.[3]

Analogies are always dangerous in this kind of argument, but this whole concept is so important to Teilhard's vision, that a simple one might serve. Occasionally a toy-shop will display a large and elaborate building made of thousands of Bayco bricks. The building is utterly dependent on the capacity of the simplest units to fit together. The tongue-groove, stud-hole technique is essential and makes the castle possible. A child might be inclined to treat the bricks as individual entities, like dominoes. But soon, by playing around with them, he would find that they fitted together; and he would be able to build slightly more complicated units, and from these he would progress to more sophisticated designs. There would, of course, be some unsuccessful attempts, and he might allow himself to be led up some blind alleys, but he would make some sort of building eventually. Teilhard admits that history is littered with unsuccessful attempts. The stream of Evolution has many off-shoots and eddies, but there can be no doubt that it is going somewhere.

Thus, for Teilhard, the world is bound for a destination; it is, as Pascal would have put it, embarked. There was a beginning and there will be an end; and the *logically* necessary end-term Teilhard calls Point Omega. On that point all things converge. To be sure, scientists have envisaged an end, and a necessary end, to life, because the *law of increasing entropy* requires us to believe that the universe is gradually running down and cooling off, thus throwing a giant shadow across any ultimate hopes for life in the material world. The question, then, is: can *Complexity-Consciousness* do for us what *Entropy* cannot; can it hold out hope of survival? Does there come a point where entropy, whose working made life possible,[4] can be overcome? Teilhard answers, 'Yes, let me explain.'

Whatever happened at the beginning, there was some kind of primordial *stuff*, ripped from the sun, and whirled roughly into the shape of a sphere, and cooling fast. This was Earth. Whatever the original *energy–stuff* was, it is clear that the particles combined into more complicated atoms and they, in their turn, combined into molecules, producing a mass of molten metal and rock, fluids and gases. Some of this molten mass eventually solidified. Gradually the form of the earth as an astronaut might see it emerged: land, water, and clouds; inert, but already containing future potential – the ability to re-form, when conditions permitted, in more elaborate constructions. Then at a certain point an enormous leap is taken. The 'impossible' happens. Atoms of carbon, oxygen, nitrogen, and hydrogen join up in such a way that a living cell, capable of reproducing itself, emerges from the broth brewing in the oceans. The organic has produced the inorganic: life. And life, compounded of a tiny selection of the available and so-called inert matter, becomes the most important fact of the evolutionary process. A frontier has been crossed. The way is now clear for flora and fauna. The *biosphere* has begun.

Having crossed the first of Teilhards' 'thresholds', we should pause to make some comments. Teilhard's view of evolution, like all others, is from the strict scientific point of view unprovable. It remains hypothesis. You cannot show it happening because the critical stages simply are not there. They are lost and gone for ever – what Teilhard calls 'the law of the missing peduncles' or stems.[6] Moreover, Omega Point, on which the whole evolutionary process converges is also (as he admits) equally undemonstrable to science.

Does this mean, then, that Teilhard is out of step with the findings of modern science? Is he, in other words, a loner? The answer is both yes and no, and it springs from his already remarked tendency to be eclectic, to take from other systems only those parts which suit his own. But even if he does not take over any evolutionary system lock, stock and barrel, it does not necessarily follow that his ideas are inconsistent with modern biology.

Broadly speaking there are two main lines of evolutionary thinking, one associated with the name of Lamarck, the other with Darwin. Lamarck held that new functions (i.e. new parts) develop from an organism's inner need, which constant use will maintain and develop, and which will be inherited by its offspring. To use a psychological term, the change is *endogenous*. It postulates some kind of *end* which the *need* articulates and the *change* satisfies. For Darwin, change springs from a fortuitous coming-together, an accidental coalition of elements; the changed organism survives only to the degree that it can cope with its environment. Nature selects only those organisms that are capable of surviving. Evolution, therefore, happens through *exdogenous* forces. It is a matter of blind chance.

Now chance is not as simple as it first appears. People at Casino tables in Monte Carlo may think that they are sporting with chance, but the ball ends up in a hole which is determined by strict laws of mechanics and, in principle, is predictable, due allowance being made for the resistance of the air, the force initially applied to the wheel, the friction of the spindle and so on. Most life proceeds in accordance with similar laws. But below certain levels of being, behaviour may be quite unpredictable and indeterminate. Moreover, there are *accidents*, when two sets of natural laws cross each other's path and get in each other's way. Leave a spool of recording tape near the field of an electric motor and the modulations on the tape will be so altered that the message will be distorted. The motor was behaving according to its laws; and the tape according to its laws. The accident of being placed near together caused change. In a similar way radiation could alter the genetic structure of an organism that happened to get in its way. There is mutation.

Teilhard accepted that in the early stages of evolution, this kind of chance played a critical role. 'Though capable of flexibly regulating within organic bodies the blind movement of molecules, life seems still to exploit for its creative arrangements the vast reactions which are born fortuitously throughout the world between material currents and animate masses.'[7] He would seem to have no difficulty in believing that life originated in this kind of fortuitous concourse of atoms. But he would want to add that, in view of the small number of elements involved, their abundance, and the unimaginable time available for them to get together, life emerged as a numerical necessity. There is creativity as well as safety in numbers.

It is not, however, a question of evolution being *solely* a matter of random happenings. New organisms do not develop only through accidental mutations. There is *psychic* as well as physical activity which allows evolution, through the organism's 'within', to have an eye on the main chance.

New characteristics may spring from a new need. Chance and the pressure of external forces create a favourable situation, but the opportunity is laid hold of by the organism's 'within'.

To take a not too serious model: let us imagine that millions of years ago there was an eyeless fish swimming around, living on any plankton that happen to float its way. Through a series of accidental mutations a small patch of its skin develops a sensitivity to light and acts as a primitive radar screen, indicating when it is in the vicinity of plankton and, indeed, when more mobile sources of food like small fish are in its vicinity. The stroke of luck in acquiring a crude eye is therefore used to help it survive in its environment. So far only natural selection has been at work. But, over a very long period, the fish finds that it has never had it so good, for the eye has altered its way of life, and in time its genetic structure is changed. The direction of the change has been conditioned by the fish's desire to consume smaller fish. So, though our original fish ate smaller fish because through a stroke of luck it managed to acquire an eye, in time its successors will retain the eye because they now *need* to eat small fish.[8] And they will opt to live where little fish are wont to congregate. And thus a variation, found useful to an organism, has been *selected* by some kind of inner requirement. It has also acquired a measure of freedom *in* its environment, though of course not yet any control *over* its environment.

Thus 'God' – to introduce a religious term for a moment – is not seen as giving nature arbitrary jabs, but as immanent in the whole natural process; He uses 'chance'. Evolution is therefore not a straight-line development, but the result of a series of gradual and powerful 'gropings' – what Teilhard called *directed chance*.

Directed chance produces from a very large number of material elements (that is, with poor *withins*) a smaller number of very complex groupings (that is, with richer *withins*). Thus the difference between low and high on the scale of creation is judged by the standard of *interiority* and *freedom*. In the pre-life period, *interiority* plays little part; there statistics rule; but after a certain stage it comes more and more to the fore.

Now Teilhard has to find a technical name to give to an organism's facility for grabbing its chance, or making the most of its opportunity. According to Paul Tillich there are moments of 'special opportunity' in history, when the ball lies at the foot in a way which it may never do again. These are described by a Greek word *kairos*, which he distinguishes from *chronos* or ticker-time. Teilhard, without knowing it, pairs these terms with two forms of energy: *tangential* energy (chronos) which is equivalent to clock time and holds things together on their predictable course – *the laws of science*; and *radial* energy (kairos) which springs from an organism's *within*, allowing it to make more complex relationships in a quite *improbable* way, and freeing it from *too much* dependence on tangential energy. Thus *radial* energy uses tangential energy to enrich life (in the biological sense) in a quite unpredictable way. (Whoever expected a whiff of oxygen and a whiff of hydrogen to come together as water!)[9]

Now you can begin to see where Teilhard is going. The greater the consciousness of an organism, the better able is it to turn a small amount of tangential energy into a very large amount of radial energy. 'One has to eat to think; but what a variety of thoughts we get out of a piece of bread; ... only a minute fraction of "physical" energy is used up in the highest exercise of spiritual energy; on the other hand, this minute fraction, once absorbed, results on the internal scale in the most extraordinary oscillations.'[10] The amount of physical energy used by Karl Marx whilst thinking about and writing *Das Kapital* can have been little in comparison with the explosive nature and 'psychic' energy generated by his disciples! And it is the *psychic* activity of man that gives Teilhard confirmation of his hypothesis that everything has

83

both an inside and an out, though positive science only regards the outside.

> It is impossible to deny that, deep within ourselves, an 'interior' appears at the heart of beings, as it were seen through a rent. This is enough to ensure that, in one degree or another, this 'interior' should obtrude itself as existing everywhere in nature from all time. Since the stuff of the universe has an inner aspect at one point of itself, there is necessarily a *double aspect to its structure*, . . . in every region of space and time . . . *co-extensive with their Without, there is a Within to things.*[11]

IV

So, to recapitulate, everything has its time; and there is a time for everything, determined by external circumstances and internal responses. Through this kind of interaction, at a certain moment, life separated out from the heart of matter, and from then on the progress of evolution centres on the *biosphere*, the layer of living things. Millions of years pass and 'a period of calm profusion' ensues. Insects, fishes, birds, and mammals flourish on the mountains, and steppes, and in the seas and forests. Nowhere is there any sign of human activity: no clearings, no smoke. But somewhere down in the forests there is a creature which carries within itself the main line of evolution. Only two groups of candidates qualify: the insects and the mammals. The insects are 'a multitude pathetically struggling in a blind alley'. Many of the mammals have thrown away their chances and are trapped, like the koala bear on its eucalyptus tree, by the very specialization that helped them to survive. 'Specialization paralyses; ultra-specialization kills. . . . Palaeontology is littered with such catastrophes.' There was, however, one group of mammals whose limbs were not over-specialized: the primates – apes, monkeys, lemurs. And, to the exclusion of everything else, evolution got to work on their brain, and they became the dominant branch on the tree of life. *Cephalisation*, the development of bigger brain-boxes, paved the way for *hominisation*, the gradual emergence of man.

There then followed a big gap between the anthropoid apes who were clearly not men, and creatures very much like them in appearance who fashioned tools and made fire, the predecessors of *Homo Sapiens*.

With the appearance of *Homo Sapiens* another boundary is crossed. He is characterized by his self-consciousness. 'He not only knows, but he knows that he knows.' He can make himself the object of his own thought. He can conceive of better arrangements. This ability is what Teilhard calls *reflection*, and reflective man became the spear-head of evolution. Thinking makes possible another layer above the *biosphere*, the *noosphere* – a network of conscious communication, language, and culture. The anatomical leap was not great, but with *hominisation* a new age is ushered in. 'The world finds its soul.'

How does the world find its soul? By some multi-mega-whiff of ultra-human spirit? Not at all. For that would amount to pagan pantheism. The world finds its soul through the souls of a multitude of individual men who are not slivers from some eternal All. But when individual man stands up, with his new power of reflection and ability to converge on himself, he tends to stand up as 'I', and Ego is not Person. Certainly individual man has an ego. He is a centre in himself and, in a limited sense, is known by what he arranges round himself. But when he tends to individualize himself he separates himself from others and drags the world backwards. The mistake is to confuse individuality with personality. To be fully man, the individual being must acquire personality; he must from his own centre reflect the power of the Uniting Centre which is Personal. He must go in the direction of convergence. He must advance towards 'the other'. The proper man is the one who finds his own personality by uniting with others; not just tangentially, touching the edges of others' being; but radially, that is from centre to centre. In other words, the true personality is constituted by Love. 'Love alone is capable of uniting living beings in such a way as to complete and fulfil them, for it

85

alone takes them and joins them by what is deepest in themselves.' This is what distinguishes between individuality and personality. 'At what moment do lovers come into complete possession of each other if not when they say they are lost in each other.'[12] And what is this loving energy if not a radiation from the Centre of centres, Omega?

Teilhard's thinking has now begun to drift away from positive science and in some senses becomes more speculative as he begins to speak of the sociological development of man. Whereas it is true that psychology and even myths and legends tell us something of man's being,[13] this is a world removed from the data which Teilhard called 'photographable'. However man, this most complicated of molecules, who is capable of reflecting and turning in on himself, now becomes a cell in a more complex organism; he forms the couple, families, clans, tribes, and nations. A new movement is at work, *socialisation*, and with it yet one more threshold is crossed on the way to drawing man and the world together in a single whole.

The picture is best represented by a cone. At the base is a mass of inert matter, gradually converging and concentrating on the axis in a spiral movement, where each layer has greater complexity and interiority, and so becomes denser and closer. But modern man is by no means at the apex of the cone, and it is what lies in the spiral above, the future, which interests Teilhard, and on the basis of what lies below, following the lines of convergence, he begins to predict what lies ahead: the development of a higher species. There is, however, a vast problem. Increasing complexity means an increase of freedom. Man can trace the story of evolution so far, can discern where it may be going, but is under no obligation to take the option of groping towards higher stages of being. He may refuse and mankind would then stabilize itself. In theological terms, he can sin. So some kind of carrot is necessary, some goal to which he can strive, and for the achievement of which he can immerse himself in reseach.[14] Thus, as well as being logically necessary as the end-term of a process which is irreversibly going somewhere, Teilhard's Omega-point begins to fulfil emotional and moral requirements. Omega is vested with personality and eternity, for man, who has personality, is not likely to give his all to the impersonal and ephemeral. Thus the world is seen to be converging on a Centre which is both Personal and Eternal.

At a critical stage, therefore, Omega 'invests himself organically with the very majesty of creation' in the Person of Christ. He, too, is part of the human phenomena. 'The Christian fact stands before us. It has its place among the other realities of the world.' Indeed he is more; he is not some added-extra. 'He is the Alpha and Omega, the Principle and the End, the foundation and the keystone. . . . He is the one who consummates and the one who gives consistence to all things.'[15] The incarnate Christ is Love, 'the love that moves the sun and all the other stars' (Dante) unconditionally suffusing every stage of evolution, and summing up all *things* (atomic, organic, mental, and spiritual) – in fact a new quality of Being initiating a new layer, the *Christophere*, and a new process, *Christification* by which the material world will be absorbed into its Final and Eternal End. 'At the very heart of the social phenomenon, a sort of *ultra-socialisation* is in progress. It is the process by which "the church" is gradually formed, its influence animating and assembling in their most sublime form all the spiritual energies of the *noosphere*.[16]

Thus, for Teilhard, the only dynamic capable of pushing evolution forward, is discovered by faith in Revelation; this is Christ the Evolver, the organic axis of whom is the church (i.e. the Roman Catholic Church!). But the church seen not as an ark from which to seek shelter from the evils of the world, but as a springboard from which to plunge into every part of the world of matter and so *Christify* the earth. Ethics, therefore, receives a new definition and a new power: to grope, though not without pain and disappointment, towards that greater unity, *planetisation* – the drawing

87

together of all nations into one – the unity to which Omega points, and which Christ commands.

Teilhard envisages an end to historical time, the Second Coming, or the Pleroma, when the Christifying of the world will be complete. In a manner which is difficult to understand, and which seems to owe a great deal to Platonism,[17] Teilhard describes how the material world will be pulled through the apex of the cone to emerge in a spiritual universe. 'The end of the world: the overthrow of equilibrium, detaching the spirit fulfilled at least from its material matrix, so that henceforth it will rest with all its weight on God Omega. . . . However convergent it be, evolution cannot attain to fulfilment on earth except through a point of dissociation.'[18]

Does this mean that the material world, once it has served its purpose in projecting a unified mankind into the world of spirit, will fall back like the stages of a rocket motor, and be consumed? 'The brew which is being boiled up is there for the very purpose of the spirit which is distilled from it, and the rest can go back on the compost heap.'[19]

If so, it looks as though Teilhard has gone back on some of his earlier ideas which spoke of eternal qualities in the physical world. In any event, the idea has served his purpose. Tangential energy is hereby overcome, the law of increasing entropy outwitted, and the 'death-barrier' broken through.

In the whole of *The Phenomenon of Man*, Teilhard speaks only of positive forces. This is partly because he was trying to speak the language of men who did not share his Christian assumptions. He did not think it necessary to show the negative side, the shadows, the abysses which, he says in a short addendum, must be obvious enough. Evil is scarcely mentioned, and when the manuscript was sent to Rome, the Holy Office was quick to spot it.

NOTES

1. *The Phenomenon of Man*, pp. 296–7.
2. Book 16: 17.

3. *The Phenomenon of Man*, p. 264f.

4. Had it not been for the law of increasing entropy, the conditions favourable to the development of life could never have been brought about. The earth had to cool first.

5. Even at the time of Pasteur it was axiomatic that the organic could not evolve into the inorganic.

6. If, for instance, after some future Ice Age, archaeologists dug up several jet aircraft, the chances of their finding Frank Whittle's prototype would be minimal.

7. *The Phenomenon of Man*, pp. 148–9.

8. Ibid., pp. 148ff. and very important footnote. In some respects this was an inspired guess on Teilhard's part which biology now tends to confirm. Cf. Ian Barbour in *The Teilhard Review*, Vol. 3 No. 6, pp. 3–6; also Alistair Hardy, *The Living Stream*, Collins 1965, p. 208; and Dobzhansky, *The Biology of Ultimate Concern*, Rapp & Whiting 1970, pp. 125ff. The critical passage in Darwin's *Origin of Species* is pp. 75–96 (Everyman 6th edition).

9. *The Phenomenon of Man*, pp. 60–64. There is an illuminating treatment of the two energies in some essays by H. A. Blair in *Teilhard Reassessed* (ed. A. Hanson, Darton, Longman & Todd 1970), spoilt only by the fact that he gets the terms confused. If we correct his use of terms, tangential energy is associated with *quantity* and Hegel's system; radial energy is associated with Kierkegaard, who called for *inwardness* and *intensity* (quality). Cf. also David Riesman's two terms in *The Lonely Crowd*: outer-directed and inner-directed.

10. *The Phenomenon of Man*, p. 64.

11. Ibid., p. 56.

12. Ibid., p. 263.

13. Cf. Richard and Eva Blum, *The Dangerous Hour*, Chatto & Windus.

14. *The Phenomenon of Man*, pp. 278ff.

15. *Science and Christ*, p. 34.

16. *Let me Explain*, p. 98.

17. Cf. especially *Phaedo* and *Phaedrus* where perfect knowledge and perfect love are able to break away from the ties of earth.

18. *The Phenomenon of Man*, pp. 287, 283.

19. *Teilhard Reassessed*, p. 83.

5 'It's "No" to Everything'

By the time Teilhard was able to return to France, in 1946, the manuscript of *The Phenomenon of Man* had already been with his superiors in the Jesuit Headquarters in Rome for more than two years. But permission to print had not been forthcoming. This silence confirmed his suspicion that in Rome he was still a marked man, and did little to revive his drooping spirits. The years of isolation in Pekin imposed first by the Sino-Japanese War and then the World War had left his body tired and his mind jaded. Pierre Leroy, a Jesuit biologist who during the exile had become one of Teilhard's closest friends, relates how life had become 'a kind of agony for him. Not because he couldn't travel, but because he couldn't meet his friends, and he couldn't exchange his big ideas with all the people in the States and in Europe.' So when he left China for good he was in the same mental state as when he first set foot there. He was very depressed and frequently on the verge of tears.

But when he returned to Paris he found that he was treated as something of a hero. His scientific reputation had gone before him. He was associated with the discovery of Sinanthropus. Some people warmed to him because he had been the victim of reactionaries in Rome. Enough of his ideas had leaked through for him to be looked upon by progressives as a real force in propelling the church into the modern world. All this, together with his natural charm and gentleness, made him 'sympathique'.

He made his home in the Rue Monsieur at the Headquarters of the Jesuit journal, *Etudes*, which acted as a focus for Jesuit intellectual life in France. In his small room overlooking the quadrangle he was able to receive old friends and new enquirers. As news got around that he had returned he found himself in great demand for retreats and conferences and, as far as restrictions on his activities allowed, he embarked on a big programme of lectures. Within a few months he had recovered his old buoyancy and was revelling in his meetings with the cultural élite and the atmosphere of the salons, and radiating an optimism which nothing was able to suppress.

There was not very much to be optimistic about. Apart from his own personal predicament, the state of the world did not present a picture which induced hope in the future of man. Europe was in ruins. The world, far from uniting, was gradually dividing into two apparently irreconcilable power-blocs. Revelations of what had happened in Germany seemed to indicate that the growth of a dense *noosphere* did not necessarily produce progress and that, under certain conditions, evolution can be speedily set in reverse. Hiroshima and Nagasaki were still on men's consciences and the shadow of the nuclear cloud was spreading across the whole world. But Teilhard refused to be daunted by anything. One of his visitors at that time was the British actor and author, Robert Speaight. 'Everyone else was plunged into despair at this new threat to the human race, but Teilhard was buoyant with optimism. I can still hear his voice saying, "Il faut croire. Il faut croire. We must believe that everything will work out for the best." '

Whilst realizing the destructive might of the H Bomb, Teilhard hailed it as a splendid end-product of human energy. Whilst the atomic tests were being carried out on the island of Bikini, he wrote an article for *Etudes*[1] which drew out the consequences of man's new power. He argued that atomic energy represented such a vast quantitative change in power that it could not be simply seen as an extension of man's tool-making ability, but as the herald of a change of plane in human consciousness. Now that man was able literally to change the face of the earth, there had been triggered off a long chain of reactions which had virtually made a new being of him. He was handling primordial energy. Teilhard had a feeling of exaltation at the way in which the explosion demonstrated the truth and beauty of mathematics. For the first flash in the Arizona desert proved to the scientists that their vastly complicated series of sums had worked out right. 'Not only could matter be expressed in terms of mathematics; it could be subjugated by mathematics.' But more important than that, the pressures of war had impelled men to achieve in three years what in normal times might have taken a hundred. This was a result of the 'largest number of brains being enabled to join together in a single organism, the most complex, and the most concentrated, for the purpose of research'. This proved that nothing in the universe could ultimately hold out against the convergence of human energy, and opened up enormous possibilities, if only men could be enthused by some goal and find courage equal to their opportunities.

Teilhard went on to say that atomic fission is at heart just the rearrangement of matter, and the rearrangement of matter in the field of molecular biology could result in a total reorganization of the human organism: the genetic control of sex and heredity, hormone processing, changing human personality by psychiatry – all sorts of prospects loomed up. But so did problems – boredom, for instance. What was going to happen to all the energy that atomic power would soon replace? Teilhard saw clearly that boredom would be one of the really big issues of a technological society, and suggested that people should be encouraged to use their leisure time for more research. He also saw that by giving man his first taste of 'super-creativeness', the possession of atomic power would shock the nations into finding some grounds for greater unity, whilst at the same time posing for everyone the question, 'To what end?' 'The final effect of the light cast by the atomic fire into the depths of the earth is to illumine within them the over-riding question of the ultimate end of Evolution – that is to say, the problem of God.'[1]

92

The prospect of Teilhard wandering round conferences in a dog-collar saying things like this must have filled some of his more conservative brethren with dismay, and one may imagine their misgivings: 'If he advocates interfering with nature by altering genetic maps, before you know where you are he will be proposing birth-control clinics for members of the Legion of Mary!' Teilhard's prospects for biological engineering, coupled with his vast enthusiasm to get on with the future, have led some people to criticize him for his latent totalitarianism. If he is touched by it at all it should probably be put down not to latent fascism but to residual Platonism! In fact it is clear from his writing that he really had no time for any system which did not safeguard the individual person. Writing in the United Nations symposium UNESCO he went so far as to suggest that any Charter of Humanity should preserve three fundamental principles:

1. The absolute duty of the individual to develop his own personality;
2. The relative right of the individual to be placed in circumstances as favourable as possible to his personal development;
3. The absolute right of the individual, within the social organism, not to be de-formed by external coercion but inwardly super-organized by persuasion, that is to say, in conformity with personal endowments and aspirations.[2]

The foundation of UNESCO with its headquarters in Paris gave Teilhard the opportunity of mixing and talking with some of the most eminent thinkers in the world. Several of them, like Julian Huxley, became his personal friends. Of course, Teilhard was now himself a man of some consequence in his own field and his peers conferred on him the country's highest academic honours. He was made a director of the National Centre for Scientific Research and was elected to the Academy of Science. He was moved by the recognition which these accolades represented and accepted them with grace and humility. But they were backward-looking and did not give him what above all he wanted: a platform where he could propound the Idea. Suddenly such an opportunity opened up. The Professor of Palaeontology at the College de France relinquished his Chair. He was his old friend, the Abbé Breuil.

It is not easy to say what Breuil thought of Teilhard at this time or whether, indeed, he thought him a worthy successor. There is no doubt that he considered him a fine person, but he had from time to time expressed some reservations about Teilhard's knowledge. He thought, for instance, that it was deficient in the history of primitive tools. Nor did he approve of him sticking his neck out on philosophical issues. And his broadcast review of *The Phenomenon of Man*,[3] though appreciative, was also cautious. Once, when comparing the two of them, Breuil said, 'Mais, je suis une gloire de l'Eglise' – the implication perhaps being that Teilhard was not a credit to the church.[4] Certainly Teilhard looked upon the possibility of succeeding Breuil as a fitting crown to his career. But he must have realized at the same time that, even if he were nominated, the chances of getting approval from his Order were impaired by his ambiguous relationship with the church. He was nominated, however, and though from the College's point of view he could have been inducted, Teilhard could not accept until he had received a reply from his Order. No reply came. He had to be content to wait and see what would happen, filling in his time as best he could with writing and lecturing within the limits of the proscription imposed on him.

No doubt amongst his listeners and readers there would be some clerics who were only too happy to detect deviationist tendencies. They did not wait in vain. Some of them would still subscribe to a *fixist* view of creation and want to anathematize anyone who both expounded evolution and quoted with evident approval the views of such well-known agnostics as Julian Huxley. These were probably not large in number, and not important. Others, with more justification, would be worried about the evolutionary slant Teilhard was giving to orthodox doctrines. Catholics had been brought up to accept a rigid division between matter and spirit, and to believe that spirit is breathed into man by a mysterious process. Teilhard's view was that, before the facts of modern science, such a distinction is meaningless. 'We must accept that man is born in his entirety from the world – not simply his flesh and blood – but his incredible capacity for thought.'[5] Thus spirit is a part of nature, and man's spiritual qualities emerge through perfectly natural processes.

The most consistent hostility to Teilhard's ideas appears to have come from people who were disturbed by what he had to say about the nature of evil, original sin, and man's freedom. Now it is perfectly true that Teilhard tended not to speak about evil. The only reference to it in *The Future of Man* is in one footnote. This is partly because he was trying to get his message across to people who had no religious background, and *evil* is a theological concept. But the main reason was that, in his view, as we shall see in a moment, the *problem* of evil did not exist. This does not mean that he was insensitive to its presence or to the suffering that ensued from it. Not long after his return to France he wrote an introduction to the biography of his sister Marguerite.[6] She had died in 1936 having been marked from her youth by sickness which she had borne with remarkable courage. 'An overplus of spirit born from a deficiency of matter.' It is very short, under three pages, but it is to be counted amongst his best writing. Indeed, it would be hard to find anywhere a more powerful and moving description of the spiritual use of suffering.[7] It is also a paradigm of his attitude to evil, and we can isolate these points:

yes, there is suffering, and its amount is directly related to the extent of 'consciousness' and thus to man's freedom;

it is extremely diverse, ranging from physical torture at one end of the scale to moral agonies at the other, and if this 'astronomic mass' were measured, it would probably outweigh the amount of joy in the world;

as man becomes more and more human, his sensitivity to the presence of evil increases and the more of a problem does it become;

but once you accept the fact that evolution proceeds on a zig-zag course, sometimes running up blind alleys, *making mistakes* and unprofitable arrangements, you begin to see evil as the by-product of the process, a wastage of energy and effort;

evil is therefore a natural consequence of the method by which life is being evolved; life is 'paid for by a large percentage of failures'.

but this wastage can itself be used as a raw material (a kind of spiritual dung!) It depends on man's attitude. It can destroy him or make him. He can suffer creatively by accepting evil, and by the principle of love he can transform the loss or wastage into spiritual gain;

so, though evil is a negative factor in life, it can be made to play a positive role by forcing man out of his self-centredness and giving him the opportunity of aligning himself with the re-creative powers which centre in Christ.

So, for Teilhard at least, the origin of evil is no mystery, and therefore no problem. It is part of the necessary process of *cosmogenesis*. He says elsewhere 'from the distant reaches in which life appears to us, it has never succeeded in rising except by suffering, and through evil – following the way of the Cross.' He was therefore able to look upon monumental evil, like the World Wars, as a crisis in growth – a deep trough before a higher wave.

Michelangelo, so a story goes, was asked once how he went about carving a head of Christ. He replied that he saw the head of Christ already existing in the stone and it was a matter of chipping away the unwanted material. Teilhard proclaims that the world will be in a process of continuous change until Christ-Omega is liberated. It is therefore in a state of continuously-being-arranged. And it is inevitable that, as the world gropes its way forward there will be waste, failures, disorder. In this light 'evil itself, in all its physical and moral forms, is no longer an intolerable affront to our reason; it is inexplicable as the residual disorder inevitably mixed with the order which is taking shape within us; and it is justified as the resistance every synthesis meets, proportional to its sublimity, in realizing itself.'[8] Or again, '. . . evil is . . . a secondary effect, an inevitable by-product of the progress of a universe in evolution'.[9] Though God *was* before time (that is, creation) he is immersed in the process; he becomes 'a particle in a world where disarrangement and disorder are a necessary part of the evolutionary process. He plunges into error and suffering to overcome them'.[10] So evil is waste, wasted energy, whether it be in a deadly virus, which is an unprofitable arrangement of matter, or the immorality of a man who does not freely choose to assist the forces making for a world converging on Christ-Omega.

There is no space here for a long treatment of Teilhard's views on evil, but you can see that many Catholics would be incensed at the suggestion that the church (with its long history, its saints, scholars, martyrs, and volumes of canon law) was doing nothing more than cope with a by-product! He seems to undermine orthodoxy at three points.

1. If evil is the necessary by-product of a God-ordained evolutionary process, then man has the burden of responsibility for evil lifted from his shoulders and it is placed squarely on God. Hitherto evil, springing from man's freedom to sin, was thought to be the cause of disorder. According to Teilhard, it is the other way round. So far there has never been any perfect order, no Garden of Eden (and therefore no Fall). Original sin turns out to be some sort of cultural lag. And even if you say that there comes a time when man's consciousness and freedom is such that he can cause evil by dissenting from *groping for the next higher plane* of being, this too can be explained in terms of psychic disarrangement.

2. Though Teilhard writes Atonement into the process by immersing God as a unitive element continually at work in cosmogenesis, the stature of the Christ-event – the life, death and resurrection of Jesus – is considerably diminished. It becomes exemplary of something which is happening all the time, and is not the once-and-for-all transaction that orthodox theology holds it to have been.

3. If evil is the necessary waste ensuing on the production of good, Teilhard is in danger of introducing an Hegelian dualism (where nothing can exist without its contradiction) and finding new grounds for an old heresy.

The great merit of Teilhard's notion is that evil is no longer a necessary hindrance to belief in God. Moreover, in holding that evil, though waste necessarily produced in the evolution of good, is none the less raw-material for soul-making, he may find orthodox support. 'Sin is behovely, but all manner of thing shall be well.'[11] But it is difficult to believe that Teilhard, in regarding evil merely as evolutionary fall-out, had really done justice to its depth and extent. It sounds too simple to be the final word about its origin. If it is, then orthodox theology cannot take him into its system and must be completely reconstructed.

Part of the reason for Teilhard's under-estimation of the power of evil was that a great deal of his thinking stemmed from an examination of his own consciousness. And he was a very good soul. He was never heard to speak disparagingly of anyone. Pierre Leroy, who knew him better than most, once told him that if he met the Devil he would say, 'But he's not all that bad.' It is not therefore surprising that after mooting an apparently superficial view of evil, Teilhard was in 1947 banned from writing philosophy, and instructed to confine himself to technical articles. When the news came to him he was barely capable of writing anything. Two months previously he had collapsed with a severe heart attack and was rushed to a nearby hospital where for several days he hovered between life and death. These were two bitter blows, but Father Barjon, who was with him at the time, testifies that Teilhard took them with 'neither bitterness nor revolt – just a child-like confidence that in the providence of God the truth would prevail'.

When he was well enough to travel he spent some time at his brother's place at Les Moulins in the Auvergne, – 'a large house full of old tapestries and pretentious arms, but perfumed with age and full of old noises'. He knew it and the surrounding country well for before his exile it was there that he made his annual retreat. Now he was content to bask in the autumn sunshine, writing a few letters, and making notes for his personal testimonial, *The Heart of Matter*.

The ban on his philosophical writing was not as bad as it at first appeared – at least in intention if not in effect. Paradoxically, it was imposed for his protection! Rome was full of rumours of heresy hunts, and a scholar, well thought of in high places, had published *A Defence of Theology* in which he urged that the works of five religious should be put on the *Index*. Teilhard was not one of them, but was told to stop publishing philosophical articles in case he should be the next; in which case all his works would have been blacklisted. This was some comfort but did not brighten the prospects that his Order might back his candidature for the Chair at the College de France. When nothing had been heard by the autumn he decided to make a trip to Rome himself to see whether he could do anything to help his cause – 'to twist the tiger's whiskers'.

As well as approval for his application for the Chair, he also wanted permission to publish *The Phenomenon of Man* and *The Divine Milieu*. He realized that there might be difficulties about *The Phenomenon of Man*, but expected none with *The Divine Milieu* as some years earlier the scholars at Louvain had 'vetted' and passed it for immediate publication.

This was his first visit to Rome. He was not moved by its ancient buildings (apart from St Peter's which he described as 'the terrestrial extremity of an arc stretching between man and what lies beyond man'); he was 'immunized against any shock'. He lodged at the headquarters of his Order with the official writers, 'the archive rats'. They were a heterogeneous group, mostly Spanish, but he found them all cordial and kind. When at last he saw the General, he was immediately won over by his honesty, directness, and humanity. But the atmosphere surrounding the Curia was stifling to thought, intellectually suffocating. Some eyed with suspicion anyone tainted with evolution and, notwithstanding the friendly reception he was given in some quarters, he felt lonely and isolated. He pined for the freedom of China and was glad to get away.

Awaiting his return to Paris at the Gare de Lyon was Mademoiselle Jeanne Mortier, a woman he had met at one of his retreats. For many years she had acted as his secretary and to her he entrusted his unpublished manuscripts. When she met him from the train, to give him breathing space, she talked for a few moments about general things. Then she said, 'Well?' He replied, 'It's "No" to everything.' He was palpably distressed, but shortly afterwards said that if his writings were from God they would survive; if they were not the only thing to do would be to forget them.

Teilhard was now convinced that his Order wanted to forget all about him and would have liked him quietly to disappear. It was clear that the authorities were not going to approve of his taking the Chair because, whatever kudos the Jesuits might get from his appointment, it would be outweighed by the ready-made and regular audience he would have for the exposition of his heterodox views. Teilhard felt they were trying to suppress him and this was confirmed when, shortly afterwards, the Editor of *Etudes* told him that he could not accept from him articles of any sort.

Academics, however, took different views. Teilhard was much in demand at the Sorbonne, where Piveteau arranged for him to conduct a series of seminars. He was elected to the Institut de France. This mark of distinction touched him greatly, but inwardly he was heartbroken and, still not completely recovered from his illness, seemed at times to be overwhelmed with depression.

With no certain future ahead of him, he went to South Africa with George Barbour, who had been one of his trusted colleagues in China. He was now seventy-two and the film George Barbour made shows him aged and frail, but the eyes-down-hammer-ready posture which was characteristic of his early years is still there. And there can be no doubt that, whatever the 'forces of diminishment' were doing to his body, his mind was as nimble as ever for he made one or two original contributions to the anthropology of South Africa. He attributed pebble-tools to the *Australopithecines*, who were then still regarded as apes by many scholars, and suggested that the widespread distribution of these artefacts showed that the *Australopithecines* were scattered over a wider area of Africa than had hitherto been thought.

Meanwhile some of his friends had been at work trying to find a *niche* where he could spend his last years, and whilst he was in Africa he heard that something had been arranged. Whilst writing to the Father-General to inform him of his plans, he took the opportunity of telling him that he would no longer try to propagate his ideas, but simply confine himself to gaining a deeper personal insight into them. He confessed that since childhood he had been dominated by a profound feeling of 'the organic realness of the world' which, with the passing of the years, had become a compelling sense of the universe's convergence on itself, which coincided at its zenith with 'Him, in Whom all things consist and Whom the Society has taught me to love'.[12]

II

The new job was in New York at the Wenner Gren Foundation. Teilhard called it his 'perch' because he did not like to think of himself as being permanently exiled from Paris.

He was no stranger to New York, having been there from time to time to attend conferences. Gradually he had come to like it and he took an almost childish delight in the neon lights and moving advertisements of Times Square. But he saw it as something more – as an example of *complexification*: as an enormously condensed and heavy human molecule, a *bloc* of mankind.

It is in New York, perhaps more than anywhere else, that you may see what Teilhard meant by human convergence, and the possibility of some future Super-man, not as a single being who is bigger and better and brainier, but as a social being in which the psychic energies of a multitude of men have evolved into a greater whole. There are ways in which this is already happening on a world scale. Isolated states and countries can no longer exist. Economic interdependence is essential. A strike in the docks of Canada affects the Englishman's breakfast. Political interdependence is a fact. But, within the limits of these necessities, states are free to develop their own individuality. So there begins to emerge a picture of a world-body in which the veins and arteries supplying economic life to the cells are the sea and air routes, the gas and oil pipelines, and the electricity grids; and a network of nerves is woven by the telephone and cable wires and the ether. Teilhard was even able to trace in the United Nations Organization the rudiments of a world-brain!

He was excited by the drive of American science and technology, with its infectious aura of 'we'll get it licked . . . no problem', and when he was shown one of the triumphs of this spirit, the cyclotron at the University of Berkeley, in California, he immediately saw beyond its capacity to accelerate physical energy to its human counterpart. It was the result of a 'spiritual tornado' that has 'just burst upon us and swept us up'. He saw cyclotrons, computers, electron-microscopes and all the other impedimenta of research as a 'fantastically variegated fauna' spreading itself over the face of the earth – all products of the 'whirlpool' of research:

Before my bewildered eyes the Berkeley cyclotron had definitely vanished; and in its place my imagination saw the entire noosphere, twisted back upon itself by the wind of research, forming but one single, vast cyclone, whose specific effect was to produce, instead of and in place of nuclear energy, psychic energy in a continually more reflective state: and that is precisely the same as saying to produce the ultra-human.[13]

The vision gave him a deep sense of peace and joy, for he could see that the 'whirlpool'[14] of research was producing an axis in its centre and was drawing mankind upwards and ahead by creating a positive pole of super-life to match the negative pole of death. Research thus pointed more and more to a divine centre and, in so doing, became tinged with forces normally inimical to science: faith and worship. He claimed that science and technology have an essentially spiritualizing role to play in life and are the ground of a higher form of adoration. They are, moreover, at root the means of carrying out the God-appointed task of subduing the earth and renewing it. Work, which is only an extremely complicated form of a very simple principle (the rearrangement of matter) may become an instrument of *Christification*.

Now that he was safely out of the way in New York, where he was virtually unknown, Rome could begin to take a more friendly attitude to him. He was invited to take part in a symposium on evolution at the Catholic University at Fordham in New Jersey. But he was still barred from Paris, and it was not until the summer of 1954 that he was allowed to revisit it. He was still a 'draw' (though some of his detractors used the occasion to mount a smear campaign) and his lectures were crowded. But the old magic had gone. The applause was polite. He was clearly a man under severe stress and the sparkle and fire had gone.

With Father Leroy he made a quick visit to see the Lascaux caves and his native Auvergne, visiting the house and the parish church at Orcines. 'I shall never see Sarcenat again.' Then he embarked for New York to face a future 'of darkness and exile'.

NOTES

1. *The Future of Man*, pp. 140–8 (Fontana ed., pp. 145–53).

2. UNESCO 1949, pp. 88–9; *The Future of Man*, pp. 195–203.

3. ORTF, 21 November 1955.

4. A. H. Brodrick, *The Abbé Breuil*, Hutchinson 1963, p. 166. The whole book is an interesting commentary on Teilhard by someone who is clearly not a convert.

5. *Human Energy*, pp. 24–8. Cf. also *The Vision of the Past*, p. 35: 'Is it not true that every day innumerable human souls are "created" in the course of an embryo-genesis so continuous that no scientific observation will ever find the smallest break in the chain of biological phenomenon?'

6. By Monique Givelet, Editions du Seuil, Paris 1954.

7. This shows how much Augustine he had 'forgotten'!

8. *Human Energy*, p. 111.

9. *The Activation of Energy*, pp. 260ff.

10. Ibid., pp. 261ff.

11. *The Revelations of Lady Julian of Norwich*.

12. Leroy's Introduction to *Letters from a Traveller*, p. 42.

13. *The Activation of Energy*, p. 356.

14. This is one of Teilhard's most confusing images: cyclones draw things up, while whirlpools suck them down!

6 'I go to meet him who comes'

Teilhard returned from France in a melancholy mood. He knew that his lectures had not lived up to the expectation of the audiences, and that in many respects he was now a spent force. Even so he realized that the chance of spending his closing years in France was quickly disappearing, and it was in Paris more than any other place that he wished to be. The 'son of all the Earth' who had spent the greater part of his life with no fixed abode found that one fragment of the world was moving in on his spirit to claim him for itself. There was a slender chance that he might be allowed to return to attend a geological congress arranged by Jean Piveteau the following year, but the Provincial would not hear of it. So he settled down in New York to living a fairly circumscribed life, bounded by the Ignatian House on Park Avenue, the Wenner Gren Foundation a couple of blocks away, and the Natural History Museum on the other side of Central Park.

He had had some success in getting the Wenner Gren Foundation to put up a large amount of money to carry out anthropological work in South Africa, the political overtones of which meant that he had to proceed with great tact. And then he turned his mind to a long cherished task: the setting up of a special foundation to explore the place of Man in the whole story of Evolution, with special reference to the part played by religion. The staff of the Wenner Gren found him an amiable companion even though they did not share his enthusiasm for the subject. And he found the work congenial. He organized a consultation or two; but the project never really got off the ground.

He was lonely, though from time to time people like Julian Huxley and André Malraux visited him, and he had several friends in New York like Helmut de Terra's wife, Rhoda, who had accompanied him on one of his South African trips, and Malvina Hofmann, the sculptress. His fellow Jesuits liked him and he was very popular in the community. Father Gannon, his superior at the time, found him 'a kindly self-effacing character', and was particularly impressed by the way he accepted his 'cross' – the refusal to allow the publication of his books because – wonderful euphemism – 'the orthodoxy was not quite clear'. 'Many other men would have given up, but not Teilhard, for he was a very real religious. If he started off on what I used to call his lyrics – something about St Paul and the Omega, I would frown and Teilhard would smile and change the subject.'

Even so, Teilhard made some (for him) biting remarks about the church, and especially about Rome. 'I have stifled in that sub-human atmosphere for fifty years.' He accused the church of shackling Christianity whose real enemy he held to be its official guardians. These comments focus on what is one of the most puzzling features in the thought of Teilhard: his inability to apply his own methodology and the test of his own Idea to the institution of the church itself. But, though he was manifestly uncomfortable in it in one sense, there is no doubt that its offices nourished his spiritual life, and he never seems to have doubted the principle of its authority or the basic rightness of its structure.

This reluctance to apply his concepts to the church as a manifestation of *socialisation* did not spring from prudence, as well it might in the circumstances; nor from his ignorance of the history of churches which were not obedient to Rome. It was not even that from being a tiny child he had been brought up to believe that the church was the only mediator between God and the world and he could not get it out of his system. (He had succeeded in getting rid of the saccharine sentimentality about the saints which had been his staple diet as a boy!) No, he genuinely believed that religious thought could develop only in a framework of tradition, and that the truth needed to be institutionalized in some kind of cultus. Wherever he looked he could find no other institution or group which possessed sufficient vital energy to be capable of lifting mankind one stage higher up the ladder of evolution. For him, as we saw, *ultra-socialisation* focused itself in the church.

A sort of ultra-socialisation is going on in the heart of the social phenomenon; in it the Church is gradually developing, as its influence animates and brings together in their most sublime form all the elements of the noosphere; the Church which is the consciously Christified portion of the world; the Church, the main focus-point at which the affinities meet that link men together in super-charity; the Church, the central axis of convergence, and the exact meeting point that emerges between the universe and Omega Point.[1]

Thus, if we go back to the example of the cone in which consciousness gradually converges on the apex, the church becomes an inner cone 'gradually uplifting the rising mass of the world, and converging concentrically towards the same apex'.[2] And Teilhard had no doubt that the axis of the cone passed right through Rome and the Pope sat on it. He was always thankful that he had the good fortune to be born into the centre of that 'specially favoured zone'. Nor did he doubt that only the Roman stock could give the biological push to bring about the massive transformation for which he was looking. He even believed that Councils and Popes were permanent organs of unification!

For a man who had spent the whole of his life dealing with the history of organisms he appears to have been very reluctant to test the church's mechanisms to see whether they were really alive and functioning as good organisms should. There is such a thing as ecclesiastical palaeontology. Churches die, and church history is littered with fossils and dead bones which once were alive with spirit. Some of them died because the bricks and mortar which contained the spirit became an incubus; others because they adapted themselves to suit the conditions of a world which passed away; others persist in an ecclesiastical dead-end, only able to live in a special cultural and social habitat, like the koala bear. Churches, too, can suffer from the effects of a law of increasing entropy when too much energy is expended in keeping the institution going, or can get trapped in their own tangential energy (canon law, institutions, quasi-religious social customs) so that any radial energy generated (like the worker-priest movement, of which Teilhard approved) may be dissipated uselessly. Church history would also point to places where, within the main stem, a group with an energetic 'within' has seized its moment and, by breaking away, has brought a new organism to life. Perhaps Teilhard was too much the victim of his models. You cannot draw a morphology of the spirit on the same basis as the Tree of Life. Branches from the main stem may yet converge! The image of the tree and cone is misleading. But perhaps if we had pressed him he would have agreed with St Augustine that the church is not only compounded of Christifying elements, nor need it be the only mode of Christification. Sometimes Christifying organisms spring up by spontaneous generation to meet a practical need without necessarily relating to any structure. Perhaps Teilhard would have admitted that he was wrong in holding that the church is the only institution providing the necessary lift, and other organizations may be unconscious agents of the redemptive process. He as good as said as much when he spoke about research and technology approximating to adoration. In any event it is unlikely that he would have held that the only way to Christ-Omega is routed through the Vatican and St Peter's Square!

These are guesses. What is absolutely certain is that Teilhard was a good religious and a devoted priest. Visitors to St Ignatius house frequently caught a glimpse of him pacing up and down the garden reading his office or saying his beads. They noted that he had become more clerical in bearing, but in what one described as a state of 'pre-beatitude'. They were impressed by the range of his awareness and his actue intelligence, by his grasp of essentials, and by the force of his judgments. But what struck them most of all was his disarming modesty and complete absence of bitterness about his fate. He never regarded himself as being better than anybody else, and he admitted that what claims to distinction he had came from a combination of accidents: birth, upbringing, environment and a combination of educational influences. But it is equally clear that he was convinced that he had been given a prophetic insight and a vision equal to the needs of the hour and the life of contemporary man. He saw himself as the prototype of a new being in whom the love of God and the love of the world were combined. What astonished him was that he appeared to be unique.

'In me,' he wrote, in what was virtually his last testament, 'in me . . . the fusion has come about – too feebly as yet for an explosive propagation – but still in sufficient strength to show that the reaction is possible and that, *some day or other the two will join up*. One more proof that the truth has only to appear once, in a single mind, and nothing can ever again prevent it from invading everything and setting it aflame.'[3] The language was again that of rhapsody, like that of St Paul, but there can be little doubt of the orthodoxy of his vision:

As mankind emerges into consciousness of the movement that carries it along, it has a continually more urgent need of a Direction and a Solution ahead and above, to which it will at last be able to consecrate itself. Who, then, is this God of the old Cosmos but the God of the new Cosmogenesis – so constituted precisely because the effect of a mystical operation that has been going on for two thousand years has been disclosed in you, beneath the Child of Bethlehem and the Crucified, the moving Principle and the all-embracing Nucleus of the World itself? Who is this God for whom our generation looks so eagerly? Who but you, Jesus, who represent him and bring him to us. . . . Lord of consistence and union . . . 'evolver' and 'evolving' . . . are henceforth the only being who can satisfy us.[4]

Few Christians would want to demur from this vision, in so far as they could understand it, but many would want to ask penetrating questions about the individual notions which go to build it up, and Teilhard had an opportunity of testing these when, in the autumn of 1954, he was invited to join a symposium of some seventy notable thinkers meeting to talk about the unity of human knowledge. People like Niels Bohr and Julian Huxley were there. So was the great historian of scholasticism, Etienne Gilson, and Protestant thinkers like Reinhold Niebuhr and Henry van Dusen. This was probably the first time that Teilhard had come up against Protestant theologians of any consequence. He was soon conscious of a deep cleavage in the gathering and was horrified to discover that the other Christians were 'either unwilling or unable to entertain the idea of a bio-logical ultra-evolution of the human'. He accused them (wrongly) of being 'immobilist'. No verbatim transcript of the discussion appears to exist, but it had all the ingredients of a crackling confrontation.

Reinhold Niebuhr was then at the height of his power. Not many years previously he had published *The Nature and Destiny of Man*[5] which cut at the foundations of liberal optimism. He had exposed the pride and sin hidden behind man's goodness and progress and, in the light of Freud and Marx, he had restated the classical doctrine of original sin. With passion and a stream of facts (and a style of speaking more frequently found in vacuum-cleaner salesmen than theologians!) he had shown that all human achievements and institutions are necessarily flawed, and that man's very creative vitality is also the means of his downfall. Far from seeing the Kingdom of God as a historical possibility, he had claimed that what makes the Christian ethic continuously relevant is its continuous impossibility. Teilhard must have listened to him with despair, and to Niebuhr Teilhard must have sounded like a voice from the nineteenth-century enlightenment.

Nor can Teilhard have found much comfort in van Dusen,

though he took to him as a person. For van Dusen was tinged with Barthianism which maintains that any attempt to find God in the natural world is of the devil, and insists that all communities and cultures stand under the continuous judgment of God. Teilhard would have to reckon with the other side of St Paul – his insistence on justification by faith alone and a rotten fig for works. If Teilhard wanted to align himself with the Paul who exclaimed 'that I may know God', he had to come to terms with the fact that Paul himself had re-phrased the exclamation, 'Nay, rather that I be known of God.'

If Teilhard found himself under fire from the heavy guns of Protestant theology, there was no refuge where he might confidently expected to find it: with the historian of scholastic philosophy. Etienne Gilson, whilst admitting Teilhard's pellucid sincerity, suggested that he had not sat down and studied the hard facts of doctrinal history, and tended to interpret some ideas of the Fathers in terms of his own. Gilson also dismissed as superficial one of the main arguments in Teilhard's case: that the masses had deserted the church because of the church's intractable inability to accept the palpable truths of science.

Teilhard seems to have been unabashed by this rough handling of his Idea, and came away more confident than ever that he was right, having seen more clearly where his effort should be directed. But he was saddened a few weeks later to hear of the death of Le Roy, in dialogue with whom the Idea had been nurtured and brought to light. 'I still think something was born there, and even though it is buried under several feet of earth, the seed will germinate.'[6] Nothing could dampen his enthusiasm. One of his friends described him as 'over-confident in the organization of his thought'. What astonished him was that so many distinguished men with the same evidence before their eyes were blind and that he was 'the only one to have seen'. So he strode on, confident that the world would ultimately be saved by the pioneers – 'those who have nowhere to lay their heads'. He asked nothing more of God than that he should be allowed (metaphorically at least) to die by the side of the road.

II

The end was now not far off. Teilhard sensed it, and his letters urge his friends to pray that he may end well, just as thirty years before he had asked to be taught to treat his death as an act of communion. For a long time he had been meditating on the place of death in his scheme of things, for an end in the sense of *finis* struck at the very foundation of his philosophy. There had to be some element of *telos*, of fulfilment. It is not easy to pin him down on the problem, for his notions of personal immortality are bound up with the 'enspiriting' of matter. He realized that a universe that continued to function while consciously anticipating *finis*, absolute death, the void, would be a monstrous and absurd one. But he affirmed that the universe was progressing inexorably into the Absolute, into Omega, and was guaranteed ultimate success. By its nature it was Personal, and the Spiritized Personality compounded in it was necessarily indestructible. Christ in All meant the ultimate transfiguring of all mankind into a single body and a single soul in Love.

In the spring of 1955 Teilhard mentioned casually to a relative with whom he was dining that he would like above all else to die on the day of Resurrection. Easter Day dawned bright and radiant. New York shimmered in the pale light. The flowers in Central Park blazed with colour, matching the dresses of the women in the congregation at St Patrick's cathedral on Fifth Avenue. Teilhard joined the crowds thronging there to hear pontifical High Mass. He despised much ecclesiasticism but he had come to exalt in the pomp which surrounded the 'outpouring of love on the altar'. He was feeling extraordinarily fit and his mind was full of plans for his work at the Wenner Gren. After lunch he went to a concert and afterwards he strolled through the park to take tea with Mrs Helmut de Terra. She handed him a cup but, before he had time to taste it, he fell at her feet, 'toppling over like a stricken tree'. He regained consciousness in a few moments and, after he was told where he was, he said, 'This time it is really bad.' Both priest and doctor were summoned. When they arrived it was too late. The coronary artery had been ruptured. For Teilhard 'the great and splendid adventure' was over. He had gone to 'meet him who comes'.

His embalmed body lay in the chapel of St Ignatius House on Fifth Avenue. A few important people came to pay their last respects. One or two noted a resemblance between his appearance and the death mask of Blaise Pascal. For the funeral, on the Tuesday of Easter week, only a dozen or so mourners gathered. A close friend of Teilhard, Father Breuvery (an economist on the staff of the United Nations) conducted the service, which was remarkable only for its simplicity. There was no music and no address. On the coffin there was a single wreath, from Malvina Hofmann, the sculptress who had modelled Teilhard's head. Only Father Leroy accompanied the hearse through the blinding rain to the Jesuit cemetery attached to the Novitiate at St Andrew's on the Hudson, some sixty miles from New York. When the cortège arrived there it was found that the ground was too hard and no grave had been dug. After the words of committal the coffin was left in the chapel.

Meanwhile, on the other side of the Atlantic, in Paris, a service was held for the repose of Teilhard's soul. The address was given by the Superior of the Order, Father Réné d'Ouince. He spoke of the way in which Teilhard's missionary and apostolic zeal left ordinary Jesuits amazed and abashed:

Père Teilhard was of the blood of great missionaries: a de Nobili, a Ricci setting out for unknown continents, eager to win the earth for Jesus Christ; of the blood of the seventeenth-century educationalists who aimed at bringing up the whole of Europe's youth into the faith of Jesus Christ; he emulated the founders of the Paraguayan Reductions whose ingenuous dream it was to realize upon earth our image of the Kingdom of Heaven.[7]

The Superior then went on to quote from *Le Milieu Divin* what Teilhard had to say about 'the forces of diminishment'.

Grant, when my hour comes, that I may recognize You under the appearance of each alien or hostile force that seems bent upon destroying or uprooting me. When the signs of age begin to mark my body (still more when they touch my mind); when the ill that is to diminish me or carry me off strikes from without or is born within me; when the painful moment comes when I suddenly awake to the fact that I am growing old; and above all at the last moment when I feel that I am losing hold of myself and am absolutely passive within the hands of the great unknown forces that have formed me; in all those dark moments, O God, grant that I may understand that it is You (provided only that my faith is strong enough) who are painfully parting the fibres of my being in order to penetrate to the very marrow of my substance and bear me away within yourself.[8]

The Superior could quite well have gone on to say that for Teilhard love of Death was the obverse side of his love of Life. He once wrote to a friend:

You do not yet love *all* life, *all* of the universe, to agree, once the inevitable moment has come, to diminish (in appearance) and pass lovingly into it (death). We must struggle against death with all our force, for it is our fundamental duty as living creatures. But when, by virtue of a state of things (transitory no doubt, but inevitably linked to the state of the growth of the World) death takes us, we must experience that paroxysm of faith in life that causes us to abandon ourselves to death as falling into a greater life. To love life so much, and to trust it so completely, that we embrace it and throw ourselves into it even in death – that is the only attitude that can calm and fortify you: to love extravagantly what is greater than yourself. Every union, especially with a greater power, involves a kind of death of the self. Death is acceptable only if it represents the necessary passage towards a union, the condition of metamorphosis.[9]

III

The cemetery at St Andrew's is on the banks of the Hudson, which flows not far away, green and mauvish, in its stony bed. Boulders of granite break through the top-soil and compete for attention with the rank upon rank of simple and similar tombstones. To each and to all, famous and unknown, the same mark is given, telling the name, the

114

dates of birth, vows, and death. When the weather became warmer and it was possible to dig a grave, Teilhard's body was added to their company.

Some of the seminarians had been playing football in the rain. When they returned they were told that the body of the Jesuit who had remained for several days in the cemetery chapel had at last been buried. One of them asked who he was. Nobody knew the answer. Somebody thought that he was French.

NOTES

1. *Comment je Crois*, unpublished.
2. *The Activation of Energy*, p. 149.
3. *Le Christique*, unpublished.
4. *Le Coeur de la Matière*.
5. 2 vols., James Nisbet & Co., 1941, 1943.
6. Speaight, p. 328.
7. de Lubac, pp. 268 ff.
8. *Le Milieu Divin*, p. 89.
9. *Letters to Two Friends*, p. 78.

Forward!

The present generation is the hinge of history. . . . We may now be in the time of the most rapid change in the whole evolution of the human race, either past or to come. The world has now become too dangerous for anything less than Utopia.[1]

People seem to be scenting that the world may be on the verge of a tremendous shift. They realize that something must be done if they are not to be the victims of nuclear extinction, suffocation by over-population, and ensnarement by the fascinating boredom of computer-controlled mass media. They watch politicians facing giant problems and offering comic solutions to tragic situations. They look for some kind of philosophy of hope which is radical enough to effect change, but compassionate enough to protect the priority of persons. Many of them see the church aligned with the forces of reaction, with power but no progress.[2] Others see it as part of the comedy; at best prophetic but powerless.

What has Teilhard to offer them, and especially those in English-speaking countries? For Roman Catholics a great deal, perhaps, but for main-line Protestantism on the face of it not very much. He does not produce any startling new discoveries: evolution, personalism, and a phenomenology of human society have for years been in the air we breathe. Apart from a few fundamentalist redoubts, churchmen have accepted man's humble origin in the natural world and have embraced evolution within the divine economy of grace.[3]

Moreover, his thought-process presents problems. He expresses his concepts in such idiosyncratic language that it is difficult to get his Idea on to the philosophical dissecting-table to see how it is put together. It is not easy to see how

116

he relates the universe's necessary progress to fulfilment in Christ-Omega, when he clearly teaches that there is a risk, and that unless we use our freedom the right way there will be an evolutionary 'stop'.

There are theological difficulties, too. It is perfectly possible to go shopping around in Teilhard's work and collect the whole of the Creed, but his evolutionary mysticism does not fit easily into orthodox theology. And it is useless saying, as I have heard said by Catholics, that 'with Teilhard you have the Catholic faith *plus* evolution'. Certainly Christ is central to his thinking, as he was to his devotion, and he has recovered for us the majesty which the 'Jesus in jeans, man-for-others' epoch has tended to obscure. But he appears to skip some of what used to be traditional belief about the means of our redemption. In writing redemption into the process and not making so much of the central drama of the gospels, he could be accused of making *history* or *time* the redeemer. He also appears to undervalue the part man plays in evil, and the cunning which human sinfulness uses to mask itself both from within (Freud) and without (Marx). Nor does he examine as carefully as he might why progress (more complex forms of life) breeds its own style of evil; so that a group will commit deeds that no individual member of it would dare; or why elements of potential union in the *noosphere*, like language, erode into forces of diminishment. It is not enough to argue that Teilhard was not a theologian and that it is a task for theologians to fit his thinking into their system (the Faith plus evolution), because if Teilhard is right, much of the system must go.

There are these and other difficulties but, beyond the abstract, Gallic style and almost unspeakable neologisms, the ultras and the supers, the vision remains, and it is vital for men of all denominations and none. Teilhard's genius was to reflect on diverse elements of nature, from electrons to nations, root them in the behaviour of the original stuff of the universe, and synthesize them in a single Idea: the concept of a world converging on itself. This vision is essentially practical. It gives each person a stake in the future, and it provides a meeting ground for Christians, Marxists, and others who share a common concern for the world that is going to be born. His vision is both a judgment and a call.

It judges: the modern world which sees only the immediate, exults in the instant, and languishes in the ecstatic; the politics which is geared to the main chance of the next five years; everything in our society which has not the vision to dream, and think, and plan, and act on the basis of the longer term, and therefore makes stop-gap remedies instead of genuine solutions.

Teilhard's message is therefore a clarion call. He brings home to us the truth that 'we are evolution', with its awe-ful consequences. Man is now free. No longer simply a child of nature, he cannot look for salvation by natural invention, which may work for animals, but no longer works for him. Nor can he be saved by supernatural intervention, for supernature is in him. He is therefore on his own and he must use his wits to preserve Life and improve its quality.

Whether we believe that the Kingdom of God will come in time at the end of history or not, Teilhard's message is the same: upward and forward, or man will never achieve the highest form of Life which is a herald of the End of Earth. The Kingdom of God is within you. He who stands at the End is with you in the Process. He is Love, and love is the only power which can achieve the convergence and unity of all mankind. And love, the primordial gracious gift, is there in the very marrow and tissue of the world. Therefore, build the earth.

This is the essential and abiding message of the long, thin, gentle priest who claimed to have discovered at the heart of matter the fundamental energy of that longing for unity, communion, and completion, for which the common people of earth yearn, of which psychologists and priests speak, and poets sing, and which, above all other creatures, is most marked in the phenomenon of man.

NOTES

1. J. R. Platt, *The Step to Man*, quoted in Arthur Koestler, *The Ghost in the Machine*, Hutchinson 1967, p. 313.

2. 45,000 copies of *The Phenomenon of Man* were sold in one week in the city of Mexico!

3. Cf. the article by J. Duckworth, 'Man's Origin and Place in Nature' in *Cambridge Essays* ed. H. B. Swete, Macmillan 1904. This lays great emphasis on psychic forces in human development.

Bibliography

If this book has succeeded in acting as a Primer of Teilhard's thinking, the reader may well ask where he should go from here. The answer is not simple. *The Phenomenon of Man* is a formidable work for people who are not accustomed to scientific or abstract language, and it is not advised as a first book. Four Fontana paperbacks will provide a good foundation of his philosophy and spirituality: *Letters from a Traveller*, *The Future of Man*, *The Divine Milieu*, and *Hymn of the Universe*.

BOOKS BY TEILHARD

The Phenomenon of Man, Collins 1959*
Le Milieu Divin, Collins 1960*
Letters from a Traveller, Collins 1962*
The Future of Man, Collins 1964*
Hymn of the Universe, Collins 1965*
The Appearance of Man, Collins 1965
The Making of a Mind, Collins 1965
Letters from Egypt, Herder & Herder, New York 1965
Letters from Hastings, Herder & Herder, New York 1965
Letters from Paris, Herder & Herder, New York 1965
The Vision of the Past, Collins 1966
Man's Place in Nature, Collins 1966
Writings in Time of War, Collins 1968
Science and Christ, Collins 1968
Human Energy, Collins 1969
Letters to Leontine Zanta, Collins 1969

* Also published as a Collins Fontana Paperback.

Activation of Energy, Collins 1970
Let Me Explain, Collins 1970
Letters to Two Friends, Rapp & Whiting, 1970

BOOKS ABOUT TEILHARD

George Barbour, *In the Field with Teilhard de Chardin*, Herder & Herder, New York 1965

Thomas Corbishley, *The Spirituality of Teilhard de Chardin*, Collins 1971

Claude Cuénot, *Teilhard de Chardin*, Burns & Oates 1965

Bernard Delfgaauw, *Evolution: The Theory of Teilhard de Chardin*, Collins Fontana Books 1961

Henri de Lubac, *The Religion of Teilhard de Chardin*, Collins 1967
The Eternal Feminine, Collins 1971

Christopher Mooney, *Teilhard de Chardin and the Mystery of Christ*, Collins 1966

J. Mortier and M.-L. Auboux, *The Teilhard de Chardin Album*, Collins 1966

Robert Speaight, *Teilhard de Chardin*, Collins 1967

Helmut de Terra, *Memories of Teilhard de Chardin*, Collins 1964

Bernard Towers, *Teilhard de Chardin*, Carey Kingsgate Press 1966
Concerning Teilhard, Collins 1969

In 'The Teilhard Study Library' (Garnstone Press) *Evolution, Marxism and Christianity; Science and Faith in Teilhard de Chardin;* and *Naked Ape or Homo Sapiens?* have so far been published.

OTHER WORKS CONSULTED

A. H. Brodrick, *The Abbé Breuil*, Hutchinson 1963

T. Dobzhansky, *The Biology of Ultimate Concern*, Rapp & Whiting 1970

121

Roger Garaudy, *From Anathama to Dialogue*, Collins 1967
  Marxism in the Twentieth Century, Collins 1970
A. Hanson (ed.), *Teilhard Reassessed*, Darton, Longman &
  Todd 1970
H. Hogarth, *Henri Bremond*, SPCK 1950
J. Maynard Smith, *The Theory of Evolution*, Penguin Books
  1966
P. B. Medawar, *The Art of the Soluble*, Penguin Books 1969
Lecomte de Nouy, *Human Destiny*, Longmans Green 1947

The Teilhard Review is published twice yearly by The
Teilhard Centre for the Future of Man, whose headquarters
are at 3 Cromwell Place, London SW7. The Honorary
Secretary will gladly send information about the activities
of the association and details of study-groups and other
literature.

Glossary of Terms

Amorisation *The process by which the world is gradually being drawn together into a unity through the growth of love in the human group*

Anthropogenesis *The process by which man emerged and is still developing*

Archaeology *The study of ancient societies by the examination of their buried remains*

Biosphere *The 'layer' of animal and vegetable life, especially that part which is not able to reflect upon itself*

Christify *The process by which God, through the Incarnation, redeems and offers man eternal life, and through man restores the world*

Christogenesis *The process by which Christ was formed in the world, through the mission of Israel, the Incarnation, and the community of faith*

Christosphere *The 'layer' of spiritual life in which human living takes on the quality of evolution's ultimate meaning, by centring itself upon Christ and being informed and energized by the grace of God*

Complexity-consciousness *The law which describes the way in which psychic energy organizes matter in progressively more complex forms, thus creating a greater degree of consciousness*

Energy, psychic *The power of man's free will, thoughts and affections;* radial *One of the marks of the 'within' of things which makes for more complex forms and deeper relationships; i.e. from centre to centre;* tangential *The energy which sustains things in purely external relationships one with the other*

Entropy *The law of increasing entropy shows that by losing heat the world is gradually cooling off and, therefore, running down, so that it will eventually reach a point when it can no longer sustain life*

Feminine le feminin *describes the unitive principle which is seen in human relationships but also is found in a rudimentary form at the level af atomic physics in the capacity of particles to unite*

Geology *The study of the crust of the earth and the relationship of the strata of rock to each other*

Hominisation *The process by which man as a reflective being emerged from more primitive forms of life*

Noosphere *The 'layer' of life representing reflecting man and what he achieves in the way of culture, art, technology etc.*

Omega Point *The end point of the evolutionary process which Teilhard claimed was logically necessary and, in his view, coincident with the Christ of the Parousia revealed to faith*

Phylum *This term is used loosely by Teilhard to describe any group of family or phenomena*

Planetisation *The process by which the various races and nations are becoming more and more one world*

Reflection *The capacity of man to know and know that he knows*

Socialisation *The process by which the human group develops from the couple, through the family, clan etc , until mankind as an entity which is aware of itself as such emerges.*

Ultra-socialisation *The process by which mankind is more and more absorbed into the love of Christ-Omega through the mission of the church; or the means by which the church is in a continual state of formation. Cf. p. 87*

Index of People